SOUL TRAVEL

to Find God's Love

SOUL TRAVEL
to Find God's Love

Debbie Johnson

ECKANKAR
Minneapolis
www.Eckankar.org

Soul Travel to Find God's Love

Printed in USA

Edited by Patrick Carroll, Joan Klemp, Anthony Moore
Author photo by Glamour Shots
Cover photo by Yoshio Sawaragi, Creative, Getty Images

Library of Congress Cataloging-in-Publication Data

Johnson, Debbie, 1951–
  Soul travel to find God's love / Debbie Johnson.
        p. cm.
  Includes bibliographical references
  ISBN 978-1-57043-233-0 (pbk. : alk. paper)
    1. Eckankar (Organization)—Doctrines. 2. Soul—Eckankar (Organization) 3. Astral projection. I. Title.
  BP605.E3J66 2007
  299'.93—dc22

                              2007000144

∞ This paper meets the requirements of ANSI/NISO Z39.48-1992 (Permanence of Paper).

Contents

Introduction

*H*ave you ever had an experience like this: *I woke up in a heavenly state of love. In my dream I had seen light and heard music that could only be celestial. I'd never heard anything like it on earth.*

Or like this:

As I drove down the street, I was floating on air thinking about my new job, what I would do, how it would be. Suddenly I stopped for a red light and realized I was not driving the car. My body was driving the car, but I was definitely somewhere else.

Or even this:

Though my comrades were dead, I was yet alive, looking at my body from above. I felt a love like never before and just wanted to stay there, in this great love that surrounded me like a warm blanket.

In such an experience you are aware of being in a state of consciousness beyond your day-to-day life. You may think you are dreaming or daydreaming. But you are really experiencing a form of the very natural state of Soul Travel.

And what is Soul Travel?

And what is Soul Travel? One example of it may be a near-death experience. Some dismiss these as hallucinations, but in a *Reader's Digest* (August 2003) article, "After Life" the writer describes out-of-body experiences that happened while a person was brain dead. There was absolutely no brain activity, so no hallucinations could take place.[1]

It can occur in day-to-day life or while asleep.

Yet Soul Travel is not just a near-death phenomenon. It can occur in day-to-day life or while asleep. Harold Klemp, leading authority and author of numerous books on Soul Travel, tells the story of Gladys. Gladys's father was a Baptist minister, so of course she attended church every Sunday. During services she daydreamed and went to a place of great beauty. She knew her body was still in church, but she felt like the essential part of her was someplace else. She often wondered, *What is this beautiful state of being?*

Later in her life Gladys hit some very low points. One night she asked God, "Where will I ever find my spiritual path?" *There must be something more*, she thought. Her body soon fell into a light sleep and, though no one else was physically in the room, she became aware of a man standing by her bed. He gave her a look of such compassion, love, and understanding that her heart filled with goodness.

When Gladys awoke, she found her depression had lifted. As she wondered about this in the weeks to follow, life's daily events soon brought her the spiritual path she'd been searching for. And with it, she found the way to visit heaven daily, via the Spiritual Exercises of Eckankar.[2]

Eckankar, the Religion of the Light and Sound of God, is here for anyone, of any faith, who wishes to consciously experience themselves as Soul and learn to travel into the heavenly worlds while still living on earth.

When I was young, I too was looking for a way to visit heaven. Thoughts like *I wonder what it's like to die?* went through my eight-year-old mind as I drifted off to sleep. One night I was listening to the television my parents still had on. Perry Como was singing my favorite song, "The stars belong to ev'ryone. . . . The best things in life are free."[3] "Dying has to be beautiful!" I said to myself. "There must be pretty colors that are different from those on earth—wonderful sounds and smells, unusual flowers, things I've never seen before!"

At eight, I had just been adopted by a caring couple, but I didn't feel completely at home there. Deep in myself, I knew I never would, because I was looking for my true home in the heavenly worlds. Even at eight, I knew I was more than just a body. I don't know how I knew it; no one had ever told me that.

I just knew.

When I was fourteen, my best friend told me about a book recounting a past life. My mouth fell open in amazement! I was so excited, I couldn't wait to read everything I could find on the subject of past lives. I knew I was not just a body, I was more, and I could travel into my past somehow.

A few years later, just before college, that same friend told me she had spoken with our local pharmacist, who told her that he knew how to leave his body. The search was on!

Before long, I found a book to help me understand who I really was and how I could travel outside

> I knew I was not just a body, I was more, and I could travel into my past somehow.

my human shell. That book was *ECKANKAR—The Key to Secret Worlds*, by Paul Twitchell, the modern-day founder of Eckankar.[4]

The book gave some exercises, and the author said that with Soul Travel, as opposed to astral projection, you are always protected and guided by an ECK Master, a spiritual guide and master of Eckankar. I still wasn't too sure about it; I didn't even know who these Masters were, but I tried the exercise anyway.

My first attempt at Soul Travel was nothing to write home about. Following the instructions, I stared at a bright coin. I was to stare at this coin until I felt myself leave my body. When that happened, I should hear a sound like a cork popping.

Well, I did start to leave my body, but then I got scared, pulled the covers over my head, and tried to hide! From what? I had no idea.

> I was able to shift my consciousness into what I later learned was my Soul body—a very uplifted state, a lighter, finer state of being.

That time, I never made it completely out of my body in the way Paul Twitchell had described, hearing a cork pop and being able to look at my body from the outside. However, I was able to experience shifting my consciousness into what I later learned was my Soul body—a very uplifted state, a lighter, finer state of being.

My first conscious experience of Soul Travel came some time later. I was lying on the floor, totally relaxed, listening to "The Blue Danube" waltz. Suddenly I felt myself floating up, out of my body! I was dancing, swirling, flying to the music. As Soul I resonated to the sound, and the music lifted me. Yet I didn't even know I was out of my body until my roommate arrived home and slammed the door. That sound jolted me back into physical awareness. I was grateful for the interruption—I knew then I'd been somewhere beyond this physical world.

I had many successes after that day, trying different Eckankar techniques for Soul Travel. I felt so much love during these brief experiences—my heart filled with joy beyond description. They also gave me a greater view of my life. From this higher, bird's-eye view, I could see how to handle things better. Instead of being one of the puzzle pieces, trying to find where I fit, I could be the puzzle worker and see all of the pieces at the same time.

During many of my attempts at Soul Travel, I was aware of still being in my body. Yet I was also in a higher state of awareness, surrounded by love, light, and sound. I've since learned that this expanded awareness is also a form of Soul Travel.

If I could do it, anyone can do it. Many people have. *You* can Soul Travel too!

Here's a way to begin: If you could be anywhere you desired, where would you like most to be right now? What kind of feeling does that place give you? Perhaps you want to be somewhere you could say, "I feel like I'm in heaven!" That's a form of Soul Travel. With Soul Travel you *can* be in heaven at any moment. It is the best way I've found to get to heaven while still living on earth. Find the purest experience of love you'll ever have. Visit with loved ones who have died. See the future, and explore past lives. Or just solve simple, daily problems.

Sound too good to be true?

With Soul Travel you *can* find the purest experience of love you'll ever have. Visit with loved ones who have died. See the future, and explore past lives. Or just solve simple, daily problems.

You can prove it to yourself by trying some of the Soul Travel exercises in this book. In addition to the exercises, you'll also find lots of stories and examples of how others have had success with Soul Travel.

You can prove
it to yourself by
trying some of
the Soul Travel
exercises in this
book.

The stories in this book come from people like you and me. They have all studied Soul Travel under the guidance of the spiritual leader of Eckankar, Harold Klemp. He is the world's greatest living authority on Soul Travel. Among his many books, one of my favorites is *Past Lives, Dreams, and Soul Travel*.[5] I will refer to Harold Klemp frequently as the Soul Travel expert and guide. He is a Master of the highest order, who knows how to navigate the spiritual worlds and guide others who wish to go there. There are many worlds, or planes, beyond this physical world, and through Soul Travel we can explore them all. As Harold Klemp writes:

> *Soul Travel goes beyond astral travel and mind travel, the common teachings of psychic groups. Generally, astral travel takes the individual to the next plane closest to the earth, the Astral Plane, which is the plane of emotion—the area where emotions originate. Some of the more spiritually advanced people can go on to the mental areas with mind travel. This sort of travel can take them to the lower Mental Plane, which is the Causal Plane; then to the true Mental Plane; and finally to the high area of the Mental Plane, which is the Etheric Plane.*
>
> *But only Soul Travel, which is in the care*

*and teaching of the ECK Masters, can take you
to the Soul Plane.*[6]

Do you want the ultimate adventure in life? Try Soul Travel. Try the Soul Travel exercises in this book. As certainly as they did for me, these exercises will help you open the doors to the heavenly worlds within you.

The kingdom of heaven is within you. It is yours to experience right now!

Are you ready?

The ultimate adventure in life is yours to experience now!

1

Soul Travel to Find Heaven Now

You do not have a Soul; you are Soul.
. . . When you say, "I am Soul," you are rec-
ognizing that you are indeed a child of God. You
share in the divine attributes and qualities of
God. All you have to do is recognize them. You
just need to be aware of who and what you are.

— Harold Klemp, *What Is Spiritual Freedom?*
Mahanta Transcripts, Book 11[1]

*W*ould it surprise you to discover you already
Soul Travel?

Most of us leave our physical bodies (or simply
leave our physical, mental, and emotional states of
awareness) many times during our lives. We're just
not always conscious of it.

In the classic sense, Soul Travel is leaving one's
body as Soul. Soul never dies, and as Soul we can
come and go as we please. Soul is not trapped in the
body, or anywhere else. You can prove this to yourself
by trying some of the Soul Travel exercises in this
book. But first things first.

ARE YOU REALLY SOUL?

Does it seem possible that you are really Soul—not that you have a Soul, but that you *are* Soul?

You can experience the creativity of Soul right now. Close your eyes and look at the blank screen of your mind. Now put your favorite animal there. What breed and color is it? How does it move? Make it move the way you want. Make it do something you have never seen that type of animal do before. For example, have you ever seen an elephant do a back flip? If not, try it in your mind's eye.

The animal did something you have never seen it do before, something not stored in your memory bank. How could you do that?

Soul has the creative ability to imagine. As Soul, you created the image of (imagined) the animal in your mind, then watched what was taking place there.

But imagination is not just fantasy; imagination is Soul's divine gift. Imagination is what Soul can use to fully experience life in this world, as well as all worlds, planes, states of consciousness, or levels of heaven. In the Bible, St. Paul mentions levels of heaven when he says, "I knew a man in Christ above fourteen years ago, (whether in the body, I cannot tell; or whether out of the body, I cannot tell: God knoweth;) such an one caught up to the third heaven."[2]

> Soul has the creative ability to imagine. But imagination is not just fantasy; imagination is Soul's divine gift.

WHY SOUL TRAVEL?

What are the benefits of experiencing different levels of heaven?

The stories in this chapter illustrate many benefits of Soul Travel. Who doesn't want more love, security, and peace in his life?

Soul Travel can bring divine love that surpasses any love you have ever experienced. It can bring inner peace beyond words and a sense of well-being that transcends all physical forms of security. Soul Travel can provide clear insights into any problem, challenge, or decision, whether related to finances, health, career, or relationships.

Yet the greatest benefit I have found is simply knowing that each time I lift my consciousness as Soul and reconnect with God's love, I am moving closer to the heart of God, my true home as Soul.

The ultimate purpose of Soul Travel is to take us back to the home we long for—the Ocean of Love and Mercy. This is the home of God, our Creator. The Voice of God (Holy Spirit) reaches us in two forms—as divine Sound and Light. The Sound Current calls us back home, and the Light of God lights our way.

In Eckankar we do spiritual exercises, such as the ones you'll find in this book. They help attune us to the Light and Sound of God, to lift ourselves spiritually. As Harold Klemp says:

> *There is a wave which comes from God. It is the Voice of God, the Sound Current, made up of both the Light and the Sound. It speaks to us in different ways, sometimes through intuition, sometimes through a messenger speaking for the spiritual hierarchy, like a guardian angel. Sometimes people hear a voice. They'll say, "God spoke to me," or "The Holy Spirit spoke to me."* . . .
>
> *The Holy Spirit also speaks to us through dreams.*[3]

Soul Travel can bring divine love that surpasses any love you have ever experienced.

The Light of God is spoken of in many religions, but the Sound of God is referred to rarely. Sometimes people hear an inner ringing or electrical sound and think they have inner-ear problems. They go to a doctor, but the doctor can't find anything wrong. Some of these people are likely hearing the Sound of God. It's different for everyone. It may sound like music, a choir, the ocean, bells, a waterfall, a musical instrument, or even the buzzing of bees.

Sometimes, as in Adam's dream, it's an indescribable, "heavenly" sound:

> In a dream I was walking home in the wilderness. It was a desolate place along a dry creek bed, with a raw reality about it. I came over a knoll, and there was a deer in the path. I felt like I didn't want to disturb it, I wanted to wait for it to cross. I saw this as a gift.
>
> Then I walked behind a thornbush. It seemed to be partially in my way. But I heard an angelic, *heavenly* sound coming from this thornbush. It was alive with songbirds! I realized the birdsong, too, was a gift of God's love amidst the dry desolation and thorny obstacles sometimes experienced in life.

The Sound of God is God's love calling us home, letting us know where to go and how high to climb.

You Can Soul Travel in Your Dreams

Adam had this Soul Travel experience in a dream. This is also known as dream travel. In it, he received a gift of God's love through seeing the Light of God and hearing the Sound of God as well. The Sound of God is God's love calling us home, letting us know where to go and how high to climb.

We can sing a love song to God, to help us connect with the divine Light and Sound. This love song to God is also an ancient name for God, known since the misty dawn of time. It is just one simple word, *HU*, sung in a long, drawn-out breath. It's pronounced like the word *hue* and sung "HU-U-U-U."

We can Soul Travel consciously, through simple spiritual exercises singing this word, *HU*, as Hannah did. She found out what it might feel like to return home to God:

> I was trying a Soul Travel exercise to see the Light of God and got a wonderful surprise.
>
> When I began the exercise, I closed my eyes and sang HU. I started to imagine what it might feel like to be in the Light of God. I imagined a bright light, warm and encompassing. Then I imagined an even brighter light, whiter and more pure than the white light before it. I wondered if I could imagine an even brighter, whiter light, so pure and pristine it would be like a diamond light. That was the brightest thing I could relate it to.
>
> As I imagined the brightness of this diamond light, I was pulled into it very fast by a gentle but firm pair of arms that seemed to form out of the light. They pulled me close, pulled me into a warm and loving embrace, as if I was a child returning home from a long, arduous journey. It was like I had been through much pain and suffering, which I had! And this being knew it.
>
> The experience of light faded, yet the feeling of this great, divine, unconditional love, warmth, and security continued to surround me. This

We can sing a love song to God, to help us connect with the divine Light and Sound. This is also an ancient name for God. It is just one simple word, *HU*.

was nothing like any human love I had ever felt. It was more pure and more permanent, and definitely more unconditional. I was not loved because of what I'd done or who I was, but for who I truly am as Soul.

I knew also in that moment that I was one of many Souls, all loved equally for simply being. Upon returning home to God, I now perceived, all Souls would be loved and cherished just as I was.

EXPERIENCE GOD'S LOVE NOW

Are you ready to experience more of God's love now? Try this simple spiritual exercise:

Take a few deep breaths, then sing HU (pronounced like the word *hue*) several times out loud. Stay relaxed, and lightly be aware of any inner sounds or sights.

Soul Travel Exercise: Find Love Now

1. Find a quiet, private place where you can sit or lie down comfortably. Think of someone or something you love. Fill your heart with love. Let the feeling of love fill your whole being.

2. Take a few deep breaths, then sing HU (pronounced like the word *hue*) several times out loud. Sing it for as long as you can, up to twenty minutes. Stay relaxed, and lightly be aware of any inner sounds or sights. Notice how you feel when you are done.

Experiencing God's love is a great benefit from Soul Travel efforts. Many people find spiritual freedom as well. Such was the case with me when I kept working at it.

This Soul Travel adventure occurred between waking and sleeping, which is a very good time to try Soul Travel. The mind is going to sleep, and we are able to bypass it. As I drifted off, I would use my divine gift of imagination to see if I could be aware of leaving my body as it fell asleep. I had been practicing this for weeks, when I finally had this success:

*A*s I was lying in bed, I wondered where I would like to Soul Travel. I decided a very green grove of trees would be nice. It was winter, and I missed the fullness of the trees in spring.

So I imagined myself in a soft, green meadow surrounded by lush trees. I could see the meadow below, but I could not seem to get down to the ground! I realized I was having a Soul Travel experience, because this was no longer my imagination.

I began to fly very fast, past my precious grove. I was flying over rocks and cliffs I had never seen before, past a very interesting canyon. That was all I remembered the next morning. I must have drifted off to sleep after that. But during that brief, vivid experience, I felt an amazing sense of freedom.

It was a wonderful feeling, and for me it confirmed that I really am Soul. Thanks to this and other Soul Travel experiences, I have found a doorway to incredible worlds of beauty and freedom.

Soul Travel is not always that dramatic. It may only happen dramatically once in a lifetime, perhaps to remind a person that he is more than just a body.

> Thanks to Soul Travel experiences, I have found a doorway to incredible worlds of beauty and freedom.

Soul Travel often happens so quietly and subtly we
don't even know we've had the experience. We most
often Soul Travel in our dreams, as in Adam's story
above. Did you ever wake up and say to yourself,
"That dream was so real!" Well, it probably was.

SOUL TRAVEL EXPERIENCES
ARE UNIQUE TO EACH OF US

Soul Travel is a very individual experience, unique
to each Soul. Sometimes it can be as subtle as a
temporary shift in consciousness, with eyes wide
open. Jeffrey had such an experience:

> *I* was driving down the highway one Thanks-
giving Day, trying to decide whether or not
to attend a second Thanksgiving gathering of
friends. I didn't need to eat more; I was very full
from the first meal! However, I wanted to visit
these dear and special friends.
>
> Would they be offended if I visited and didn't
eat anything?
>
> I was thinking about this, and how much I
loved these people, when I saw an eagle soaring
overhead. Instantly, it seemed as if I was about
ten feet away from this magnificent bird. I could
see the golden sunlight shining through its tail
feathers and gleaming off its white head. I could
see every detail of the eagle's body. I was filled
with joy at this gift from God, this closeness to
such an incredible being.
>
> That was how I felt about the people I would
be visiting. I decided this was a definite sign
from God that I should go. Of course I was warmly
welcomed, hungry or not.

We most often Soul Travel in our dreams. Did you ever wake up and say to yourself, "That dream was so real!" Well, it probably was.

Later on, as I told the story of the eagle, I realized I had actually been out of my body. There was no other way I could have felt so close to the eagle and seen such detail. Also, it seemed like time stood still: I felt I was there, close to the eagle, for minutes, when it couldn't have been more than a split second.

How Do I Know If Soul Travel Is Real?

How do you know if your Soul Travel experience is real?

Harold Klemp explains it this way to members of Eckankar:

> *You're going to have many different experiences on the path of ECK. Some of them will be as dynamic as anything you've ever experienced. Others will be like a dream. And some will be simply like figments of your imagination.*
>
> *A test of an experience is: if it helps you open your heart to divine love, to God's love, then it's a real experience.*[4]

Only you can tell. It is an inherent sense you have as Soul. Deep down, you will know.

In time, and with practice, it will become clear to you what's real, what opens your heart to God's love. Meanwhile, no one can question you if you don't tell them about it. Often it's best to keep these experiences to yourself. People who do so may find they have more of these special experiences.

Would you like to begin experimenting to find God's love through Soul Travel? Let's see what our Soul Travel expert, Harold Klemp, recommends:

A test of an experience is: if it helps you open your heart to divine love, to God's love, then it's a real experience.

> *Most people . . . are unaware that there is something beyond our everyday life, beyond this physical universe. . . .*
>
> *If you are not aware of what is happening to you in the dream state, in the invisible spiritual worlds, you are not living your life fully out here in the physical world. . . .*
>
> *The Spiritual Exercises of ECK are the key to these inner worlds. They are the key to your secret worlds.*
>
> *The Spiritual Exercises of ECK are simple. For example, . . . close your eyes, at home or in some quiet place, and sing HU to yourself.*[5]

Soul Travel can be as simple as a shift in consciousness. Yet however it is done, whatever experience takes place, it helps us find God's love here and now. This love comes from the inner planes, or heavenly states, into our outer lives, showing up in many different forms.

Soul Travel can be as simple as a shift in consciousness.

CAN SOUL TRAVEL HELP PEOPLE HEAL?

People receive the blessings of God's love in many different circumstances. These blessings often come from experiences that lift us above the physical world. For Kristen, it was a dream-travel experience in the form of a healing:

I've had this knee problem for the past four years. I ran track in high school and pushed myself too much. Ever since, I've always had knee trouble. Four years ago I developed a chronic limp. I was always in pain, but it was something I'd just grown accustomed to.

Then I had a dream where my spiritual teacher, the Mahanta, was looking at my knee. After the dream, my knee didn't hurt! I thought my knee was healed in my dream, but I kept thinking, *It's not possible, it's not possible.* All morning it felt normal, like my other knee. Yet it was more than I could accept as possible, so the pain returned.

I sometimes get to this point where if something is really, really good I won't accept it or even acknowledge it's there. That was the case with this miraculous healing. Finally, I realized I just needed to accept it.

Another dream occurred, this time with many friends around me. They were all giving me love. My knee healed once again, and this time I could accept it.

The dream state is very real for me, and the experience of healing proved to be real—both in my dream, as a real spiritual experience, and in my waking life, as a much-improved health condition.

Kristen referred to the Mahanta, her inner spiritual teacher. The Mahanta is a very special teacher, a spiritual guide who works with anyone who asks. He will not interfere in anyone's life. He is here to help guide Soul back home to God. He is a guide and a coach for the journey into inner worlds, the many levels of heaven; he can take you safely and directly past the rocks and snares, because he has been there himself. He has been through everything in the world and everything in heaven to be here now as a spiritual guide and teacher. The present-day Mahanta,

The Mahanta is a very special teacher, a spiritual guide who works with anyone who asks. He is here to help guide Soul back home to God.

the Living ECK Master is Harold Klemp.

There are other ECK Masters who assist the Mahanta, the Living ECK Master, the spiritual leader of Eckankar. To learn more about these ECK Masters, read *Those Wonderful ECK Masters*, by Harold Klemp.[6] The Mahanta and the other ECK Masters work inwardly to guide spiritual seekers who are ready to explore new spiritual worlds. The most obvious quality people notice about any ECK Master is his or her great love. They often appear to be angelic in nature, and they can provide personal guidance and upliftment, as Diana discovers in the next story.

The Mahanta and the other ECK Masters work inwardly to guide spiritual seekers who are ready to explore new spiritual worlds.

CAN SOUL TRAVEL HELP WITH CAREER CONFUSION?

Diana had an experience with an ECK Master that helped her in her career:

I was moving into areas of greater responsibility at work—a real stretch from what I'd done before. I was dealing with feelings of low self-confidence, unworthiness, and fear.

In my spiritual exercise one day, I went to a familiar healing place on the inner planes. There was a high mountain cliff—higher than anything we have in the physical world. I would sit and look over the abyss from a park bench near the edge. I felt complete peace in the slight breeze, knowing I was above my earthly worries. Sometimes the Mahanta, my spiritual guide, would come to sit with me and talk.

This day, I sensed a presence standing nearby. I turned to see Rebazar Tarzs, another of the

ECK Masters. He said, "An eagle never thinks about falling, it just flies." As he spoke the words, an eagle soared past in front of me.

This Soul Travel experience helped me regain my spiritual sight and focus. It gave me the courage to try my wings, and I found that I could fly!

WHAT ABOUT PROTECTION FROM HARM?

The Mahanta is even more than a spiritual guide and teacher. He is also a protector. Nia had a dream-travel experience where he gave her a vital warning:

> *I* never wore my seat belt until an intense dream I had. In the dream I had a really bad car accident and died. The next day, I decided I'd better wear my seat belt!
>
> It saved my life. I had an accident that very day. I would have been killed—or so the police officer told me. My car was totaled, but I came out of it just fine. I was so excited about having been warned in the dream.
>
> The dream seemed like a real experience, which is why I decided to start wearing my seat belt. Now I trust in God *and* take the proper precautions!

Dreams like Nia's may feel like real experiences. They often are real experiences on another level of heaven. Sometimes they are a way of working out problems that we don't need to face here in the physical world. These problems are usually the effect of something we put into motion sometime in the past. This is called karma. Does it seem strange to you that we may have such traumatic experiences in heaven?

The Mahanta is also a protector. Nia had a dream-travel experience where he gave her a vital warning.

It seemed strange to me, too, until I found out that heavenly states, or inner planes, are just like earth in many ways. They still have both positive and negative energy until Soul reaches the higher planes, beginning at the Soul Plane, where there is only pure positive energy, or spiritual flow.

CAN SOUL TRAVEL HELP A PERSON THROUGH ROUGH TIMES?

Dream travel and Soul Travel can be separate experiences, or combine and blend with each other in an exquisite way. Marianne found poetry in her experience and heaven in a special moment:

I was going through a really tough time and asked for help from the Mahanta, my inner spiritual guide. I also asked for help from any of the ECK Masters.

That night in a dream, I had a wonderful Soul Travel experience with nine ECK Masters, including the Mahanta. But I did not remember it until several days later during another Soul Travel experience. Here is what happened:

I was unable to sleep one night, so I got up and tried to do a spiritual exercise. I often do a spiritual exercise where I meet with several ECK Masters at a table in the higher planes of God. These Masters may not look familiar to me, but I sometimes hear a name and will go look it up later, only to find out it is actually an ECK Master's name.

The spiritual exercise didn't seem to be working for me this time, so I tried exercising on my treadmill instead. Everything was so quiet

Dream travel and Soul Travel can be separate experiences, or combine and blend with each other in an exquisite way.

that all I could hear was the sound of the tread-mill. It was singing to me rhythmically. I then started to sing HU, the ancient love song to God. I asked the Mahanta, "What is it like to be a vessel for the Holy Spirit, the essence of God?" I didn't know if it was even possible, but I wanted to experience what it would be like to become one with It, so that I would have more compassion, love, and understanding of everything. I just wanted to experience what it would be like.

Then I felt a song or poem come to me from the inner planes. I began to sing these words:

Show me the way to the heart of God;
Teach me how to be a vessel of love and
    mercy.

I repeated these two lines again and again. Then I heard some more lines to the poem:

You dipped me in the ocean and set me free,
Told me to take a sip and just be.
The water was sweet as nectar, it cleaned me
    through;
I felt so light and so new.
I looked at you and you started to laugh,
As I realized
I was swimming in the Ocean of Love and
    Mercy.

After I sang these lines, I realized I had heard them before in a dream! The dream I'd had a few days earlier was filtering through to my conscious mind. In the dream I had met with nine ECK Masters in my special place and said one word to them: "Help!"

I felt a song or poem come to me from the inner planes. After I sang these lines, I realized I had heard them before in a dream!

The next thing I knew, I was standing with them on a beautiful seashore. They all picked me up and unceremoniously dipped me into the ocean. I was surprised to find that I could actually breathe in the water! Then they said, "Take a sip." I felt cleansed by it. I thought the water would be salty, but it tasted sweet.

Feeling happy and refreshed, I looked up and said, "Where am I?" One ECK Master answered, "The Ocean of Love and Mercy," and they all laughed.

My request had been answered. And the answer had been given days before I even asked the question!

An interesting side note: I thought I had been on the treadmill for about five minutes, but it was actually forty-five minutes. I had definitely been out of my body!

WHAT ABOUT COMMUNICATION WITH LOVED ONES?

Sometimes Soul Travel involves communicating with our loved ones. Annalisa's experience was dramatically positive, loving, and heavenly. Notice the transition from dream travel to Soul Travel:

Sometimes Soul Travel involves communicating with our loved ones. Annalisa's experience was dramatically positive, loving, and heavenly.

was in a new relationship, and my boyfriend, Jim, and I had to be apart for Christmas. Before we left on our separate trips, I said to him, "Let's meet on the inner planes while we're on vacation."

One night I had a dream with him where I heard the song "Unchained Melody." I woke up still feeling as though I was with him and he was hugging me. It was the most wonderful hug! My whole body was warm and full of love. It was unique because it started in that in-between state, between sleeping and waking, but then continued when I was fully awake. It was as real as any experience I've ever had. I could feel him right there with me.

Then I called Jim, and he told me the exact same thing had happened to him! It confirmed that this relationship was special and that we had a strong, loving bond.

Jim and I have now been married twelve years. I still get inner confirmation when he's thinking about me: I hear our special song, "Unchained Melody."

That Soul Travel experience really made an impact on me. It showed me you can really meet people Soul-to-Soul, that it's real.

Via Soul Travel, we can even communicate with loved ones who have passed on. Sylvia had a special gift of inner communication with her grandmother who had recently died:

Via Soul Travel, we can even communicate with loved ones who have passed on.

When my grandmother died, I missed her very much. I asked the Mahanta, the Dream Master, to help me visit with her in the dream state. I knew this was possible from my studies in ECK. I had a dream where I was a little girl sitting on her lap. It was my way of giving her love.

I was able to use the spiritual tools I've learned to go beyond the physical world, to make a connection with that Soul who was my grandma. What's interesting is that I was grown when she died, and taller than her. Yet I could be a little girl in the heavenly worlds and sit on her lap. Love knows no boundaries.

Indeed, love is expansive, beyond time and space. But it can also be tricky, especially when it comes to human, romantic love.

CAN SOUL TRAVEL HELP
WITH RELATIONSHIP ISSUES?

Brent found a way, with Soul Travel, to navigate love's potentially stormy waters:

*W*hen I used to meet someone attractive at a party or elsewhere, I would become infatuated and emotionally involved very quickly. This used to get me in trouble and into relationships that went nowhere.

Now that I know about Soul Travel, when I meet someone I like I step back from the experience and do a Soul Travel exercise. I look at the situation from a higher point of view, which is what Soul Travel is for me. I can almost play the relationship along the Time Track like a video. I do that by asking myself a question like, If I was in a relationship with this person, where would it go?

If I were to look at the potential romance from an emotional point of view, like I used to, it would always feel really good; I'd soon be planning our life together in my imagination, including marriage and babies! But from the Soul point of view, I can ask questions without getting so emotionally attached. Among other things, I ask, What lessons would I be learning? Is it going to be good for me spiritually, or will it hinder my spiritual unfoldment? I may not need to repeat old lessons. Perhaps I would only be building unnecessary karma.

Now I look at the situation from a higher point of view, which is what Soul Travel is for me.

If it feels good and looks good spiritually, and I can see a spiritual benefit, I go ahead with pursuing the relationship. But I still keep checking in on the inner planes through Soul Travel.

Even if the relationship is hard or it ends, I can see the lessons I learned.

Brent is finding heaven here and now—running a smoother life and looking for the spiritual lessons in all of his experiences. Would you like to try a Soul Travel exercise to practice Brent's method?

> Even if the relationship is hard or it ends, I can see the lessons I learned.

Soul Travel Exercise: Relationship Overview

1. Look at any relationship you are considering entering into, whether it be friendship, romance, or business.

2. Ask the Mahanta (or any spiritual teacher you follow) to go with you and guide you on this adventure. Or simply ask for guidance from God. Imagine yourself in the future with the relationship you are considering. How does it look and feel to you?

3. Jot down any notes about what you saw or felt. Refer to your notes later.

Relationships at work may fall into troubled emotional waters too, and Elly found a cure:

I had a boss with a volatile temper that triggered an old pattern of fear. He would walk up and just blast me with anger. It would make me physically sick. I was literally sick to my stomach with anxiety. I didn't want to be the effect of his anger or my fear anymore.

I asked the Mahanta for help in the dream state. In my dreams I would see my boss and would actually do nice things like hug him! I felt love pouring from me to him. This was amazing to me. The Mahanta was using love to dissolve my fear. Love is stronger. The love helped me become free of the fear. It was a slow process for me, taking about one year.

My dream travel had obvious outer results: My boss didn't come around me much anymore, nor did he get so angry. Eventually, I found another wonderful position doing a job I love.

Elly's solution was graceful in the highest sense. Love indeed is the most powerful force of all, and it can show up anywhere. Animals often exhibit this great gift from God.

CAN ANIMALS SOUL TRAVEL?

Animals are Soul too, as you may have guessed if you've ever been close to a pet. The following story shows Soul Travel in both humans and animals:

Animals are Soul too, as you may have guessed if you've ever been close to a pet.

J had a really powerful Soul Travel experience when my rabbit died. I was very close to Mi'jo, and he was a tremendous vehicle for love and healing in my life. I knew he had been sent by God.

I used to hold Mi'jo cradled in my arms like a baby, and he would relax and go out of his body. His head would flop back, and when he got back in his body, he would lightly jerk awake in my arms.

SOUL TRAVEL TO FIND HEAVEN NOW

Mi'jo got sick one day, and I was very concerned because when rabbits get sick they can die very fast. I wanted to be there with him if he was ready to die. I left the house only for a short while. He still seemed OK when I got back and checked on him, though he was still sick.

I wanted to be sure he didn't die alone, so I put him beside me in bed. At one or two o'clock in the morning, I woke up and got a strong inner nudge to pick him up and cradle him in my arms. This time when he left his body, he didn't come back. It was a blessing for us both: He didn't have to struggle to die, and I was holding my beloved rabbit.

While I was holding Mi'jo for the last time, inwardly I was having my own Soul Travel experience. I saw the Mahanta on my right side and Prajapati, an ECK Master who works with animals, standing right in front of me. I handed Mi'jo to him. This whole experience was very beautiful and filled with love. Then I came back into my body and knew my rabbit had died.

I was thankful to the Mahanta and the Soul who was my rabbit for letting me be a part of this. It would have been hard to just find him gone in the morning. This way, I could see that he didn't have to suffer, and I was able to witness his transition into the next life.

Soul can travel back to earth as well, after the body has died. This was true for Gail, whose cat came back to let her know he was happy:

When our cat, Winston, died, I was so sad. One night soon after his passing, I heard him meow! I had been lying in bed and was half asleep, so I said, "Winston, what are you doing here?" I actually saw him too!

Then I woke up fully. Winston immediately disappeared, but the love stayed. I knew he was in God's hands, and I felt a wonderful inner peace.

God loves all of creation. And why not—God created it! Therefore, we are always loved by God. We can experience more of that love, and find heaven here and now, by practicing Soul Travel. In the next chapter you will find new ways to try it for yourself.

God loves all of creation. And we can experience more of that love.

2

A Variety of
Ways to Soul Travel

Soul Travel simply means that you as Soul
are moving into a higher state of awareness.

— Harold Klemp, *What Is Spiritual Freedom?*
Mahanta Transcripts, Book 11[1]

The easiest way to Soul Travel is to use the best-kept secret in the universe, your divine gift of imagination. Parents may tell children at a certain age, "You're too old to imagine anymore." Adults say, "That's just your imagination." The truth is that your imagination is real on some level of heaven. Anything and everything you imagine exists somewhere, or you wouldn't be able to imagine it!

Many people, including myself, first started practicing Soul Travel with the hesitant thought *That's just my imagination—nothing more.* Then something miraculous took over: the Holy Spirit. Intuition, or knowing, began bringing the gift of validation. Also, I knew I was Soul Traveling when I would get pulled back into the body by a phone ringing or some other startling noise. It was such a huge shift in experience,

> The easiest way to Soul Travel is to use the best-kept secret in the universe.

31

in feeling and being, like I had been floating and was
now hitting the ground with a splat! My imagination
had indeed taken me away to far-off heavenly realms.

PROVE TO YOURSELF THAT
YOU ALREADY SOUL TRAVEL

You can prove
to yourself that
you already do
Soul Travel.

You can prove to yourself that you already do Soul
Travel.

Think of a time you were driving or walking
along, your thoughts on something else, like who
you'd be visiting or what you'd be eating. Then, suddenly, something brought your attention back to your
body or car. You realized you'd been gone when you
said to yourself, "Oops, I'd better pay closer attention." You *were* paying attention; it's just that your
attention was being paid elsewhere!

Imagination becomes a real experience for Soul,
moving in and out of worlds that most people only
dream of, if they're lucky. And if these people could
believe their dreams were real, they would have the
second-easiest way to Soul Travel.

The following exercise is from Harold Klemp's
book *The Art of Spiritual Dreaming*[2]:

Spiritual Exercise:

Using the Imaginative Body

The imaginative faculty within yourself is like
a muscle. You're going to have to train it day
after day. What you are actually doing is learning how to become aware and observant of
yourself in a different state of consciousness.

One way is to go to different places in your imagination. Maybe you'll want to re-create a plane ride: I'm sitting in the airplane seat. What do I see? What do the people look like? What happens when I walk down the aisle? What is on the food tray?

As you go through the day, you'll find yourself looking at objects and making mental notes, because that physical information about the dresser or the clothes in your closet will be helpful when you sit down in your chair and try to visualize it for Soul Travel.

Here is an experience Jasmine had with Soul Travel using imagination:

felt emotionally upset when I woke up from the dream state. I had no reason to be upset that I knew, but sometimes dreams help work out difficult situations, even when I don't remember the dream. When I did my spiritual exercise that morning, I imagined myself at a Temple of Golden Wisdom where I could get some comfort and healing. My imagination became reality as the Holy Spirit took over.

I noticed a door open to a classroom and felt the class was for me. This class was taught by an ECK Master. *ECK* is sometimes short for Eckankar and also a word for Holy Spirit, the essence of God. These Masters often teach in beautiful buildings, called Temples of Golden Wisdom, in the heavenly worlds.

Now remember, this seemed like it was all

I imagined myself at a Temple of Golden Wisdom where I could get some comfort and healing.

in my imagination, but this is our window to Soul Travel. The ECK Master Lai Tsi was telling the class how to heal emotional stress. He then walked toward me and told me I needed to fill myself with love while I was doing this exercise. I remembered a sweet bird I had seen and heard singing that morning, and the memory filled me with love. I began to see golden drops of liquid love begin to rain around me! It was wonderful, and I felt so much better.

Would you like to visit a Temple of Golden Wisdom in the heavenly worlds, as Jasmine did? Try this next exercise.

> Imagination is our window to Soul Travel.

Soul Travel Exercise:

Visiting a Temple of Golden Wisdom

You may want to look through the Eckankar booklet *ECK Wisdom Temples, Spiritual Cities, & Guides: A Brief History* as an inspiration for your journey.[3]

1. Notice something that fills you with love. Hold that feeling in your heart as you continue this exercise.

2. Think of something you would like to know spiritually. Imagine there is a class going on right now at a Temple of Golden Wisdom that can answer your question.

3. Imagine what a Temple of Golden Wisdom might look like, and imagine yourself walking into it. Imagine yourself in class, with an ECK Master

or whomever you look to as your spiritual teacher. Imagine what he might say to you in regard to your question. Write anything that you remember when you return.

Imagination Is the Key to Many Worlds

Imagination was used in a most interesting way in this next Soul Travel experience. Jillian accepted an assignment for her writing class that would help her soar creatively, and as Soul:

At a recent professional writer's conference I had an awesome experience. One teacher gave us a writing exercise that would forever change the way I viewed writing and start me on my writing career in earnest.

The instructor showed us a picture and told us to "travel into it." I focused on imagining I was the person I saw in the picture, to write from that view. Suddenly it was very real, as though I had been pulled into the picture and it became alive. I became that person with all the emotions and thoughts he would have. I just couldn't believe how easy it was to write from that perspective. I couldn't even believe it was happening!

I know that when actors prepare for a specific role, they have to study their character to become that character, with all that character's thoughts and feelings. That's what this experience was like. I became the character I imagined through Soul Traveling. I'd heard that editors are always looking for the most well-developed characters in books they consider for publication.

> I just couldn't believe how easy it was to write from that perspective. I became the character I imagined through Soul Traveling.

This experience gave me the means to develop my characters more fully and put me on the path to my writing career. I finally felt ready.

Because I practice the Spiritual Exercises of ECK daily, I had the spiritual "muscle" to easily slip into the experience the teacher gave us.

Why not try the exercise Jillian was given to help stimulate your imagination?

Soul Travel Exercise:
Imagine Yourself There

1. Find a photo or painting that you love, and imagine putting yourself into it.

2. Write about the scene—what you are doing there and how you feel. Does it become real for you?

Mimi's story reveals a secret to finding God that is emphasized by the ECK Masters—opening the heart to love.

As we will see in the next story, Mimi's spiritual exercises gave her some spiritual "muscle" as well. Her story reveals a secret to finding God that is emphasized by the ECK Masters—opening the heart to love:

started dancing when I was nineteen years old (that's very late for serious dancers to begin studying). After obtaining a degree in dance through a university in Germany, I went to New York City to advance my studies in ballet. I wasn't sure how I would be able to support myself with dance, but Holy Spirit kept me going; that and my love for dance, which opened my heart to God's love. My inner guidance was so strong to continue.

I practice my spiritual exercises regularly, and dance is one way I feel I am also doing a spiritual exercise. I had one experience that confirmed this for me.

I was about to be videotaped dancing onstage, so I did a spiritual exercise to prepare myself. My inner teacher, the Mahanta, was there. He asked me inwardly, "Why do you dance?"

I answered, "For all that is life, and to bring as much love and beauty down here as I can." Then inwardly I went onstage and started to dance. I started moving onstage, then was out of my body in dual consciousness (aware of both the physical body and myself as Soul). There was a six-pointed white star that started in my heart and built up to a column of light. There was so much love! I was amazed to see that it was so real now, it took on a life of its own. I did not even wonder if it was my imagination, because it was absolutely real.

I stopped the contemplation (spiritual exercise) then because the light was so strong. I was awestruck. I was almost scared, so I dropped out of the experience in that moment.

Before this experience, I had wondered how it would be to feel worthy. Even though I stopped the experience, I had my answer. If that's how it feels when I do what I truly love, then this is what I truly am as Soul. I don't need to feel more worthy. Being worthy or not doesn't matter.

If we are that much a vehicle for the Holy Spirit when we do what we really love, then we are a Co-worker with the Holy Spirit, with God,

When we do what we really love, then we are a Co-worker with the Holy Spirit, with God.

already. I also learned you can use anything that opens your heart as a spiritual exercise.

You can try Mimi's technique:

Soul Travel Exercise: Go for the Love

1. What do you love to do with all your heart? Is it golf, tennis, quilting, horseback riding? Perhaps you simply love walking in nature. Pick one thing that you love doing, and focus on being there in your imagination.

2. Open your heart to the essence of what you love about that activity. How does it make you feel? What special gift of Divine Spirit is in it for you?

3. Let yourself ride the wave of divine love that it brings to you.

Love and gratitude open the heart and help to replace any fear.

Love and gratitude open the heart and help to replace any fear about Soul Travel.

CHALLENGE YOUR INNER EXPERIENCES

Just a note here about any inner experience that doesn't seem right: Always challenge any inner experience you have that doesn't feel like God's love.

Here's one way to do that. Sing HU, the ancient love song to God, and say, "I challenge you in the name of the Mahanta" or "in the name of God." See what happens. Trevor challenged an experience he had, and it kept him from making an expensive move:

I was thinking of moving back to Colorado from Wisconsin, when I had a feeling something wasn't right. My inner experiences had felt real when I thought I heard the Mahanta, my inner spiritual guide, advising me to move. Yet, I remembered to challenge this when I saw something that upset me.

I was driving down the street the very day before I was to leave for Colorado, and I saw the wing of a Canada goose lying on the road. This meant to me that I would lose my freedom if I were to go.

I then challenged what I previously had heard advising me to move. I found it had not been the Inner Master, but my own desires that were leading me. Now I heard the Inner Master clearly. In fact, it was the Inner Master that had drawn my attention to the goose wing in the road. This was not the right time for the move. I decided I would stay, and I immediately felt better.

Later, I was able to make that move when it was in harmony for everyone concerned. I was grateful for the warning that told me to take another look at my motives.

DAYDREAM TO SHIFT YOUR AWARENESS

Spiritual exercises, or Soul Travel of any kind, may reveal past lives that are affecting this one. (If you are interested in more on this subject, see my book *Exploring Past Lives to Heal the Present.*)[4] When you have a question while Soul Traveling, you may get surprising answers—even when you don't ask the question! Carrie got an answer while daydream traveling. Here's her story:

Spiritual exercises, or Soul Travel of any kind, may reveal past lives that are affecting this one.

I knew I needed to take a trip to Germany when I had a strong inner feeling I would soon be going. This would be my first visit to Europe, and I was very excited.

On the plane to Germany, a really intense anger came over me. It almost seemed to beam out of me, very strongly. This was not like me at all. Where did it come from?

The anger went away shortly after the plane landed, but I tried to find the cause of it. I had to find out what it was.

I was to be in Germany for three weeks, so I kept searching. Germany felt very familiar to me, like I had been there before. Yet three weeks went by without any clues.

On the way back to the U.S., I spoke with an acquaintance. She was telling me about a situation with her father. They were angry at each other.

Just after that conversation, I started drifting into daydream mode. All of a sudden I was remembering a past life in Germany with the same father I have now. We butted heads then as much as we do now! My mother was the same mother as well.

It was the early 1800s, and my father in that life had a desire to go to America when I was in my midteens. There were younger children in the family, and I was the oldest. My father told me I was to be left behind with two maiden aunts. They would see that I found a proper husband. My aunts were nice, but life with them could not replace the adventure I might have had going to America.

I was angry that my father had controlled

All of a sudden I was remembering a past life in Germany with the same father I have now.

my life this way. I would rather have had an adventure than be married. I didn't even want to be married!

In this lifetime, my father again made it his goal to see me married, even though I kept saying, "I don't want to get married!" That, of course, was before I met my husband.

My husband now was also my husband in my past life in Germany, and we wouldn't have met in that life if I hadn't been left behind.

This has helped me to understand where my dad was coming from this lifetime. I've been able to let go of some of the bad feelings and disagreements with my parents. I can now see that, in his own way, my dad was a channel for the Holy Spirit. Though his words seemed negative, there was a positive outcome—the one I really wanted.

I realize that my father's wishes for me did not mean compromising or losing my freedom and independence. Rather, my life has been enhanced by being married to the right person.

This has helped me to understand where my dad was coming from this lifetime. I can now see that, in his own way, my dad was a channel for the Holy Spirit.

Soul Travel Exercise:

Daydream Your Way to Heaven

1. While lying in bed awake, or while doing a simple task where your mind may wander, try looking at where your mind is wandering. Perhaps, as you are doing the dishes, your mind wanders off to the movie you are planning to see. As Soul, imagine you are there already, smelling the popcorn and relaxing into the comfortable seat.

2. As you plan your day in your mind, watch how often you leap ahead to be in the situation you are thinking of, with all of the emotions involved. Do you have an important meeting? Will you be going to your favorite restaurant later?

3. Any of the images that pass through our mind or imagination can begin a Soul Travel experience. Where do you want to go? Just daydream about it in a relaxed way. You may even say something like this to yourself: "I wonder what it would be like to be _____ or do _____." Then use that as a springboard for a spiritual experience. You are already moving as Soul, so why not go higher? For example, "I wonder what it would be like to visit my grandmother in heaven." or, "to find the most beautiful place in the heavenly worlds."

SOUL TRAVEL IN YOUR DREAMS

After you work with your daydreams, lucid nighttime dreaming may be your next challenge of interest. Lucid dreaming simply means that you, as Soul, have awareness of your dreams. You are awake and aware as Soul while the body and mind still sleep and dream. Soul is really having the experience anyway, every time you dream.

When I have focused on Soul Travel through lucid dreaming, I've had some interesting experiences, such as these two:

I was falling off a cliff, and I knew I was dreaming. Since I also knew I was on the

Lucid dreaming simply means that you, as Soul, are awake and aware while the body and mind still sleep and dream.

inner planes, where everything is possible, I made myself fly. I felt so much freedom!

In another lucid dream I was in a flooded basement. As the water started to rise, I began to swim. Soon I was underwater and breathing with no problem! Then I decided to control the water. I made it go higher, then recede until there was no more flooding. Then I brought it back in waves that took me higher and higher, into the next level of the house. This showed me how I could move into a higher level of life just by knowing I could.

In both lucid dreams, I realized that I wasn't trapped anywhere, or in any danger I couldn't escape. This made me feel invincible, helping me lose more of the fear of death.

Inner Knowingness Is a Higher State of Soul Travel

Soul *is* invincible, because It is eternal. It also has the ability to communicate to the lower self, the mind and emotions, as Barry discovered:

When I was in high school I used to hang out with a group of friends. A new boy came to our school and wanted to hang out with us. I immediately felt distrust. My inner voice said, "Don't have anything to do with him."

I tried to avoid being around him, but my friends let him in, and eventually he stole something from me. It made me realize that my inner voice was real and was from a higher source.

It is a blessing for me to be able to hear the wisdom of Soul. That kind of "knowing" is a form of

> Soul *is* invincible, because It is eternal.

Soul Travel. As our Soul Travel expert, Harold Klemp, explains so beautifully:

The classic
Soul Travel
experience is
leaving the
human body in
full awareness
and having the
Light and Sound
of God flow
directly into the
Soul body. But
some people go
on to Seeing,
Knowing, and
Being.

The classic Soul Travel experience is leaving the human body in full awareness and having the Light and Sound of God flow directly into the Soul body. But some people have done that in earlier incarnations and have no desire to go through the ABCs of spiritual school again. The Mahanta may give them a few brief refresher Soul Travel experiences, and from then on they go on to Seeing, Knowing, and Being. . . . To see, know, and be are the qualities of Soul that are at the forefront of attention in the Soul Plane and above.[5]

I had an experience of seeing and knowing when asking a simple question about a trip.

was trying to decide whether to take a trip to Tampa, Florida, for an Eckankar seminar I wanted to attend. My life was in a bit of turmoil, since I'd recently been divorced and was between jobs. I really didn't feel it was the best time to travel. But several people I knew had asked me if I was going, so I began to think more seriously about it. I decided to do a spiritual exercise and ask my inner guide, the Mahanta, whether or not to attend. After all, in his outer form as the spiritual leader of Eckankar, he would be the speaker. I opened my heart, sang HU for a few moments, and asked my question: "Should I go?"

I immediately saw the Mahanta inwardly, and he said in a booming voice (very unusual for me to hear his voice this way), "Stay put!"

I asked again since this was highly unusual. I got the same answer.

Eckankar seminars like the one in Tampa are such a great gift for me. They are so full of love and so uplifting. I grow so much from each one and come away feeling like a new person. It seemed like a smart thing to do, but here was my spiritual teacher saying no. I listened and followed my inner guidance, as I usually try to do without *too* much argument.

About one week later the confusion cleared up. I decided to move to California. My inner guidance on this was just as clear as the guidance to *not* go to the seminar in Tampa. The move to California was for a short time, but it was essential for me to heal and rebuild. I needed to establish new patterns in order to move forward spiritually, and this was the most effective way to do so.

The ability to shift in consciousness as Soul and hear the inner guidance keeps me on track. I am so grateful for this gift from God that keeps my feet on the earth and my heart in heaven.

Read on! The next chapter gives more intriguing examples of ways to Soul Travel, as well as practical benefits for your own life.

The ability to shift in consciousness as Soul and hear the inner guidance keeps me on track.

3

Practical Soul Travel

As Soul, you are like a balloon that rises above the ground. The higher you go, the farther you can see. And the farther you can see, the better you can plan your life.

— Harold Klemp, *The Golden Heart*,
Mahanta Transcripts, Book 4[1]

Soul Travel can be very practical. It can be used to solve the mysteries of life, be they human or divine. All life is of the Holy Spirit. It is teaching us constantly. It is teaching lessons each Soul needs to learn. Your universe is your creation, your challenge, your puzzle.

If we have a high enough point of view, like the balloon in the quote above, we can be the puzzle workers. Rising above problems as Soul can help solve the mystery of your personal universe, making life more understandable and more enjoyable.

Soul Travel can be used to solve the mysteries of life, making life more understandable and more enjoyable.

Painful Lessons Can Uncover More Love

The experiences Martina had helped her uncover several spiritual lessons in her life and accept more of God's love:

47

*A*s soon as Gerard and I met, we fell in love. I had a strong feeling that I knew him so very well.

Before we met, a friend at work often said, "You should meet Gerard!" while telling Gerard he should also meet me. This went on for about a month until we did finally meet.

We were so in harmony, even our spiritual beliefs matched perfectly.

We were together for eight years, and life was very good. He was very supportive, and I felt so secure and loved. I was sure we would grow old together—a good, strong couple, rocking on the front porch.

I was in for a surprise.

In the seventh year of our relationship, we started bickering about nothing. Something wasn't right. We had never argued like this before. It became so intense that we talked about separating. Then suddenly the bickering eased. We still loved each other, so we tried again to make things work.

It wasn't long before the bickering started again, and a second time we decided it would be best to separate. This pattern repeated itself a third time, until finally we realized that we just had to stay apart. Maybe the Holy Spirit was trying to tell us something.

Eventually we had to separate our lives completely. This devastated me because I still had deep feelings for Gerard. I was grieving for him so much that I would burst into tears just seeing a couple holding hands. It came with a deep longing inside that was very unusual for me.

Two years went by and, while the pain had

> In the seventh year of our relationship, we started bickering about nothing. Something wasn't right.

eased, my heart still ached from this feeling of loss. I kept asking myself if I could have done something more to keep us together. And why wasn't my heart healing? All during this time, I sensed that when the time was right I would understand.

One morning I did a spiritual exercise (like the one on page 14) and saw a segment of a past life. I felt as though I was in eternity in one split second, viewing the Time Track from above, as Soul.

There was so much detail! I could see, smell, hear, and feel everything. I saw myself among villagers walking barefoot in the mud behind Gerard, who was on horseback. He was of a higher status, a noble, and I was a peasant. We were very much in love, but we could never be together openly. It would have meant prison or death. Gerard was deeply saddened that I had to walk in the mud while he rode in comfort. He was distraught that he could do nothing about it. We left that life feeling unfulfilled and longing to be together.

It all began to make sense to me. In this life, we picked up where we left off in a previous life. Gerard generously shared his material wealth and love because he couldn't do so in our past life together. He encouraged me to improve my station in this life and supported me in every way through upward career changes. We had this tremendous joy in being together, yet we never formally married. Perhaps we still unconsciously felt we were not allowed to.

A healing took place in another Soul Travel experience where Gerard and I met on the inner

I did a spiritual exercise and saw a segment of a past life. It all began to make sense to me. In this life, we picked up where we left off in a previous life.

planes. It was a happy occasion. We hugged and then turned and walked in separate directions. I felt incredible bliss, joy, and a tremendous release. I felt so happy and free that, in celebration, I gave gifts to people at work! The karma between Gerard and me was finished, and all that remained was God's love.

After this experience I understood what God's unconditional love for us is. It isn't a love that has to possess. It allows each of us to go our own way without any of the emotion from the past to hold us back in this life.

I recognized our unique need to have our own individual paths back to God. The joy and pain I experienced had strengthened my heart so I could accept this greater love.

LOSE YOUR FEARS THROUGH SOUL TRAVEL

The Mahanta is more than a spiritual guide and teacher; he is also a protector. The stories that follow illustrate this blessing. When a person experiences this love and protection firsthand, he knows he is always safe in the arms of God.

A mother's love is one of the most powerful forces in the world. Becky had hers tested and rose above fear to save her son in this dream-travel flight:

When a person experiences this love and protection firsthand, he knows he is always safe in the arms of God.

I had a dream where my small son, Daryl, and I were in a garage on a nice afternoon. I looked up and saw a huge grizzly bear at the other end of the garage.

The bear looked straight at me. He started moving toward us. I was terrified. The closer he got, the more I froze in fear. I didn't know how to protect my son. I couldn't even say anything

to Daryl to get him to protect himself, because
it was all happening so fast. So I just asked the
Mahanta, my inner spiritual teacher, to let me
be a vehicle for love. I just switched instantly
from total fear to total love, because I had to. It
was the only option I had!

As soon as I did, our eyes locked and the love
just flowed out of me and showered this bear. He
drank it in and dropped on all fours, ambling out
of the garage.

I woke from the dream and recorded it in my
dream journal. This experience was so real, I
knew it was significant.

A week later, I shared the experience at a talk
I was giving. A Native American was in the
audience. She said, "Do you know what the sym-
bol of a bear is? It's the protector." I knew then,
by the feeling that went through me, that this
was important. The Mahanta had tested me
through the image of the bear to see if I could
move from fear to love. It was a great way to know
that it was the Holy Spirit working with me.

To see how the Mahanta works with all of
his students is amazing to me.

The following is a very practical and very effec-
tive exercise to help face and conquer fears. It's from
Mary Carroll Moore's book *How to Master Change in
Your Life: Sixty-Seven Ways to Handle Life's Toughest
Moments.*[2]

Spiritual Exercise: The Fear Room

Close your eyes, and breathe deeply for a
few moments to relax any tension inside.

So I asked to be a vehicle for love. I just switched instantly from total fear to total love.

Imagine you're looking through a window into a small room. It's dark inside and filled with fog, a fog so dense that it's hard for you to make out the shapes of any objects.

Behind you is a large truck. A machine is being unloaded by some burly men. They wheel the machine up to a hole in the outside wall of the room and attach a long tube, like a vacuum-cleaner hose. One of them flicks a switch, and you watch as all the fog is slowly sucked out of the room.

Then the men unhook the machine, load it back onto the truck, and drive off.

Walk into the room, and look around. The fog is completely gone. There's a pleasant fragrance in the air and a light, pleasing sound you can barely hear.

Go to each of the five large windows in the room, and open the shades, allowing sunshine to flood in. Look around the room. What is left?

As we face our fears, we can be supported through Soul Travel—through the practice of lifting our-selves into higher states of awareness and love.

In her book, after this exercise, Mary says:

The room symbolizes the inner bodies—the emotions, the mind—that are filled with fear. Sometimes when I am facing a turning point that frightens me, I do this exercise several times a week. Each time I try it, the inner room is filled with the fog of fear. But I find that when I clean out the inner fog, my heart feels lighter.

As we face our fears, we can be supported through Soul Travel—through the practice of lifting ourselves into higher states of awareness and love. Kaya dis-covered this while relocating:

J had leased a fourteen-foot U-Haul truck to move my furniture. Now I was dreading the experience of having to drive this huge truck across several states and did not want to do it.

I'd been planning and packing for two months, so I was a little worn out even before the road trip started. I was also worried about how things would go, especially about driving this huge truck.

Yet, once we were on the road, just working with Divine Spirit cleared up all my concerns. For instance, I worried about how I would get through intersections but as I surrendered the situation to Divine Spirit, people just made way, or the intersection would suddenly be clear! I would worry about getting across the street or pulling into the filling station, and every single time, the traffic cleared!

I said to my daughter, "Do you realize how much Divine Spirit is helping me with this move?"

I know this doesn't sound like much, but it's kind of like I was in a void, where things just started coming together and I just sat there and watched it happen. This is a form of Soul Travel, because I was seeing from the Soul perspective. That's the way I experience Soul Travel more than any other way.

EVEN THE FEAR OF DEATH CAN BE OVERCOME VIA SOUL TRAVEL

Kaya illustrated a basic spiritual principle to make life easier: surrender to God's will. Not my will, but Thine be done. It's so practical! It can save a lot of stress.

A basic spiritual principle to make life easier: surrender to God's will.

Nell found that out as well, as she faced her own death head on:

've evolved from the point of expecting my imminent death to not even focusing on it! I felt like death was imminent when my cancer recurred. I still tried different therapies, but my outlook was set on preparing for death. I even chose where I wanted to pass on.

In the meantime, I worked harder spiritually. I made a greater effort to be aware of the presence of Divine Spirit. I kept up with my spiritual exercises.

As I went through the next couple of years, I asked for help from Divine Spirit to gracefully do whatever I needed to do. Divine Spirit was teaching me acceptance. If I die, I die. If I live, I live. I understand now that it's just another step; it doesn't matter where I live, whether it's here in the physical or in the heavenly worlds.

Because I knew I could be in the heavenly worlds at any time, I was beginning to see life more from the Soul viewpoint. It's like Soul Traveling all the time!

For example, now I have a different perspective on how I approach people. It's in a more relaxed, accepting way. I no longer have expectations of other people. It's not because I think less of them; it's more like a detachment that allows me to view life from a higher perspective, as Soul. I now watch what happens in my interaction with people instead of expecting the conversation to go a certain way. I let Divine Spirit run the show more often now.

I think the experience of knowing you are

> Divine Spirit was teaching me acceptance. Because I knew I could be in the heavenly worlds at any time, I was beginning to see life more from the Soul viewpoint.

terminal, that you are going to die soon, helps you understand this higher view. Opening more to Divine Spirit helps me to quiet my internal mental voice so I can be more aware in the moment. This is like a Soul Travel experience in that there's an opening up of possibilities, to experience what Divine Spirit wants me to experience. Many things that used to be important to me are now in perspective. I see things more for what they are. And death is just a doorway to a much greater life. As Soul, this is my perspective.

THE HEALING SALVE OF SOUL TRAVEL

Life's lessons are unending, yet often there are periods of healing in between, as I discovered one day:

T here was a time I felt so exhausted I didn't know what to do. I tried every healing method I could think of, going to various doctors and health practitioners who tested me for anemia, parasites, and everything else you can imagine.

One day when I especially needed extra energy to finish an important project, I decided to do a spiritual exercise to find some help. I imagined there was a temple of healing in the heavenly worlds where I could find an answer. The temple was a very light, milky blue-green color. It had gorgeous columns and a huge stairway going up to the entrance. I walked in and looked around. Then there was someone directing me toward some special baths.

This was where my imagination let go and

Life's lessons are unending, yet often there are periods of healing in between.

Divine Spirit took over. I believe the experience was real, because it certainly wasn't something I would have thought of myself. I walked to the baths and was told to step into one of them. As I soaked in this bath, I felt so much better. I knew I would be able to finish the project. This experience showed me how very real these temples in the heavenly worlds are.

Would you like to try the exercise that helped me so much?

Soul Travel Exercise: Healing Temples

1. Think of what you would like to heal in your body or emotions.

2. Imagine a temple that is just for healing. What might it look like? What colors might it be? What colors are comforting and healing to you?

3. What mode of healing seems appropriate for you? Perhaps it will be someone to listen or a massage or special bath. Take off on your own and find what's right for you.

Physical healing can also come about through information received during a Soul Travel experience.

Physical healing can also come about through information received during a Soul Travel experience, as this mother discovered:

My children were very young, and I was a single mother. I could not afford to be sick, nor did I have the time!

I went to bed feeling ill one night and asked the Mahanta, the Inner Master, for help. I had a dream where I was shown a medicine cabinet. When I opened it, there was food inside. These were the "medicine foods" that would keep me and my children healthy. These foods were good for us and did indeed help us to stay healthier. I was very grateful for the view from Soul's perspective.

DECISION MAKING WITH SOUL TRAVEL

Without solid decision-making tools, it's difficult when we can't see the future or how our plans may affect us down the road. Just as a wide-angle lens on a camera shows more of the picture, Soul Travel can give you a much broader view.

Joanna was able to see more clearly with that view and make some hard decisions that would affect her life dramatically:

> Just as a wide-angle lens on a camera shows more of the picture, Soul Travel can give you a much broader view.

I was feeling very badly about my life—really depressed due to a relationship that seemed ill-fated. I'm from Holland and my boyfriend was American.

I was not a U.S. citizen, so I had to return to Holland soon unless I got married or got a work permit. Bart, my boyfriend, was not ready to make a commitment like marriage. I was distraught and didn't know what to do. I had to make a choice between getting a work permit to stay and going back to Holland to be with my family and friends.

I decided to try a simple Soul Travel exercise (described below) and got my answer. I'm not very visual, and I don't hear God talking to me. There's no thunder and lightning, but I do get answers. They are like impressions or feelings about what to do.

This time I knew I had to go back to Holland. The exercise also continued to help me maintain my perspective through the next year.

Back in Holland, I kept in touch with Bart. I would be visiting the U.S. at Easter and was looking forward to visiting him. We planned to become engaged, but I didn't think he really wanted to marry. Again, I needed to take the higher view and see what Spirit wanted me to do.

Finally I said to God, "I totally surrender now. I'm willing to leave this man. I've had enough of going back and forth. If it's not meant to be, I'm willing to walk away."

Before, it was *my* will ("I want to marry this man!"); now it was *Thy* will be done. This was my long-awaited lesson.

Eventually Bart and I parted, but I know I made the right decisions from a higher point of view. I know my surrender has led me to a greater life of love.

Think of a challenge in your life today. Now see yourself flying as if you were an astronaut. Imagine you can see everything from a high, spiritual perspective.

Soul Travel Exercise:

Making Decisions from a Higher Viewpoint

1. First, think of a situation or challenge in your life today. Then imagine yourself leaving your body and floating above your home, then your city, state, and country. Now see yourself flying farther out, as if you were an astronaut, floating above the earth. Imagine now that you can see everything and everyone on earth in a new way, from a high, spiritual perspective.

2. Ask yourself, "What is the solution to this prob-

lem?" as if you are looking at it from the perspective of a heavenly, all-knowing being. Or
say, "I know the solution to this problem. It
is_____." (Continue the thought with whatever
comes to you as this enlightened being.)

3. Let yourself take in the answer, and look at the
   possible wisdom in it. Write down the answer
   and anything else that comes to mind.

We sometimes make decisions as Soul and don't
even know we made them! Life can be so much richer
when we listen to the Holy Spirit. That's what David
did:

> was filled with love one day and had a
> strong inner feeling to pick up a gift. I
> thought it was for a friend who was having a
> birthday. I had already gotten flowers and was
> wondering about this. Was this gift for her?
>
> My inner guidance said no.
>
> Was this gift for another friend's Christmas
> present?
>
> "No."
>
> Was it for the same friend for a special situ-
> ation?
>
> "Yes."
>
> My friend was going to be giving a talk at a
> very special worship service at the Temple of ECK
> in Chanhassen, Minnesota. I was to meet her
> backstage to help her with something, so I brought
> her this gift as well. When she saw what it was,
> she was delighted and said, "How did you know?"
>
> I actually didn't know! But evidently it had

We sometimes make decisions as Soul and don't even know we made them! Life can be so much richer when we listen to the Holy Spirit.

some special meaning to her. I didn't know mentally; but as Soul, my love had opened me to the guidance of the Holy Spirit.

EVEN FINANCES DON'T ESCAPE SOUL'S EAGLE-EYED VIEW

In Eckankar, we learn that we are unlimited in our potential for spiritual unfoldment. We can learn self-mastery in this life and go on to become spiritual masters in service to all life. Mona found out she could use Soul Travel to gain mastery even over her floundering financial state.

Mona found out she could use Soul Travel to gain mastery even over her floundering financial state.

One year ago I was teetering on the edge of financial disaster. My brother-in-law told me to file for bankruptcy. He said there was no way I could get out of my financial mess unless some huge change happened. But in contemplation, I kept getting the answer "You won't have to file for bankruptcy."

In a dream, I observed myself meditating under a bodhi tree. This was a past-life image. There were spiritual masters behind the tree. They said, "For you to understand this lifetime and this situation, you have to connect with this consciousness under the tree."

I asked, "Isn't that me?" They said, "Yes. But you have to make the connection."

As I connected with the person under the tree, I got the message that I needed to be fully responsible for my actions.

I then found myself in a Temple of Golden Wisdom, studying finance with a group of people. The Mahanta said something in the dream that I couldn't remember until I woke up. As I woke up I heard a voice say, "You cannot move forward spiritually on this path unless you take responsibility for the past. Mastership lies in self-responsibility."

So that day, mulling these words over in my head, I walked into a shopping mall and saw a sign that read Now Hiring at Dayton's. I signed up for a part-time job that I could do in the evenings after my day job. I thought to myself, "How am I going to do this?" But I remembered the statement "You must take responsibility."

Two weeks later I had a new day job as well, and my daytime income increased! Somehow, the money came very easily then, and I started to pay off my debt.

I felt a huge weight lifting from me. Other people confirmed what was happening. They would say to me, "You seem different, you look lighter."

When I was in that former life under the bodhi tree, I did nothing except focus on my spiritual self. If I wanted to move along to Mastership, I had to take 100 percent responsibility for all aspects of my life.

I had the power to change and to take control of my life. I am now two-thirds out of debt, and in just one year!

I know if I had chosen bankruptcy, I wouldn't have gotten to the place of freedom I reached spiritually.

To find a great solution for any problem, do a spiritual exercise. The following exercise focuses on the Sound of God. It is from Harold Klemp's book *The Spiritual Exercises of ECK*:[3]

If I wanted to move along to Mastership, I had to take 100 percent responsibility for all aspects of my life.

Soul Travel Exercise: The Purifying Sound

Close your eyes and look to the Spiritual Eye [just above and between the eyebrows, on the inner screen of the mind]. Sing HU, an old and secret name for God. It is one of the most powerful words for spiritual upliftment that I can give you.

As you sing HU, listen for the Sound. The Sound may be heard in any number of different ways. It can be like the sound of a train going by, a bird, buzzing bees, sometimes a flute, or even guitars. The way you hear It just depends on where you are.

These sounds are the action of the Holy Spirit, the ECK, as Its atoms vibrate in the invisible worlds. The Sound you hear is the vibration at the particular level to which you are attuned at the time.

Imagine the Sound purifying you, removing the impurities of Soul. It will bring you an understanding of how your actions have caused your problems. It will also give you an indication of what you can do to unfold and how to figure out the way to do things right.

As you sing HU, listen for the Sound. The Sound may be heard like a train going by, a bird, buzzing bees, sometimes a flute, or even guitars.

Difficult experiences can certainly reveal golden truths from God, and this motivates us to explore more of these truths. Courageous truth seekers do so every day. More brave Souls share some special Soul Travel adventures in the next chapter. Use their stories as springboards into adventures of your own!

4

Adventures in Dream
Travel and Soul Travel

The dream world is a fascinating place. As you explore the variety of experiences in the other worlds, you are expanding in your spiritual awareness. Your attitudes change. Awake, you handle certain situations differently than before. You become more diplomatic, more mature, and more responsible. These changes emerge from the experience you are gaining on the inner planes, first in the dream state and later through other methods of inner travel.

— Harold Klemp, *The Eternal Dreamer*,
Mahanta Transcripts, Book 7[1]

As Harold Klemp, the leading authority on dreams and Soul Travel, says in the above quote, dreams are a beginning step to travel in the inner worlds. They are also an easy way to see how you are already Soul Traveling. In time, dream experiences may reveal themselves as real experiences. I had one such experience with my mother.

Dreams are an easy way to see how you are already Soul Traveling. In time, dream experiences may reveal themselves as real experiences.

63

Communication with
Loved Ones beyond This Life

Because of a dream, I was well prepared for my mother's impending death. At the time, in the physical world, she was seventy-eight years old.

In the dream she was dressed in a long, sparkling formal dress, looking young and beautiful. She told me that she would not be around much longer, but not to be sad. She was happy and having a good time, showing me that she would also be having a good time where she was going after she died. She wanted me to be happy for her too.

A few months later my mother discovered she had cancer. The doctors had given her about six months to live. But, character that my mother was, she told us, "I'm not organized enough to die. Besides, I want to live to see my eightieth birthday!" She actually lived until a few weeks after her eightieth birthday party, held at her "hospital at home," where she presided like a queen.

Just a couple weeks before her death, I asked what she thought she'd be doing in the heavenly worlds. She said, "Oh, probably playing cards with the old gang!"

Happy and joyful till the end, my mother fulfilled the promise of the dream. As Soul, she spoke to me clearly so I would not be too upset. She gave me time to adjust.

Many others have had similar experiences with loved ones. Sometimes people experience their loved ones visiting them, as Soul, after death, to give assurance, comfort, and love. One woman said, "My husband died a year ago, but he still sits next to me

Sometimes people experience their loved ones visiting them, as Soul, after death, to give assurance, comfort, and love.

in his favorite chair as I watch television."

Another woman shared this after her husband passed on: "My husband and I are still playing golf in my dreams. I see him every night!"

To try communicating with a loved one who has passed on, try this next exercise:

Soul Travel Exercise: The Inner-net

1. Imagine the person you would like to visit in the heavenly worlds. Don't worry if you can't remember how he looks. Simply think of the feeling of love you have with that person.

2. Ask God or the Mahanta to help you meet with the person you'd like to see. Then imagine how the meeting might unfold. Let your imagination go, and observe where it takes you. Put yourself fully into the experience.

3. You may want to note your experiences. You can share them later with someone who knew that person. The comments or facts you record may help you value your experience.

COMMUNICATION WITH LOVED ONES IN THIS LIFE

Some dream-travel experiences, like Samuel's below, may reveal another, more loving side to someone you know who is still alive.

Some dream-travel experiences may reveal another, more loving side to someone you know who is still alive.

When I was a child, I lived with my grandfather for about five years. My impression was that he was derogatory and mean—not very nurturing. He had been very hurt, so he was usually full of anger. He didn't seem to have much love to give.

Then, when older, I had a Soul Travel experience in a dream that revealed another side of him. My grandfather was there, really young, like in pictures I've seen of him, and he was full of love! This was so unusual, not really like him. In the dream his eyes were sparkling and he was so loving. He said, "Don't ever let anyone tell you that you can't accomplish anything." That's just the opposite of what he told me when I was a child!

It was Soul speaking to Soul. These were the words of encouragement I needed to hear at the time. That it came from him was really special. Even if we have relationships that are painful, we are just Souls trying to do the best we can and teach each other. Everyone is Soul, even if we don't always see them that way.

> Everyone is Soul, even if we don't always see them that way.

FROM DREAM TRAVEL TO SOUL TRAVEL

"Dreams are a window to heaven," says Harold Klemp. *"They link the two realities of heaven and earth—and allow you, as Soul, to move freely between them every single day when going to sleep."* [2]

Dream travel can also be very therapeutic, as in Laurie's case:

I had just done a spiritual exercise before bed to help me answer a question about how to let go of control issues. Here's the dream I had:

I was on the Astral (emotional) Plane, a level of heaven, with a therapist I had decided to see. I knew she could help me let go of having to control everything so much. I saw her sitting on a bench overlooking a pond nestled in a lovely, soft green meadow. I sat down beside her to ask about making an appointment, and she began to cry. She said, "I've had such a horrible day!" and began to tell me about it. I just listened to her and comforted her, saying I knew the feeling.

I then walked home, wondering if I actually needed therapy. I was going to ask my husband what he thought.

When I woke up from the dream, I told my husband about the experience and asked his opinion. He said that maybe that *was* my therapy. Then, to illustrate, he asked me, "What's the opposite of control?" I answered, "Listening, letting her talk." Soul Travel therapy! It gave me an insight into how to let go of control with other people, and I was grateful.

Dream travel can develop into Soul Travel, especially when you practice lucid dreaming—being in control of the dream from the high viewpoint of Soul. Camille practiced diligently:

> I tried different techniques to Soul Travel in the dream state. I would wake up in a dream, but I wanted to move on to a more clear, direct experience of Soul Travel. How could I pass that threshold?
>
> I was in bed, trying to roll out of bed in my Soul body and ground myself. I put my feet on the floor and focused on being grounded. It worked, but it was a very short, quick experience.

Dream travel can develop into Soul Travel, especially when you practice lucid dreaming—being in control of the dream from the high viewpoint of Soul.

I fell right back into my body. I couldn't keep that state.

I was then dreaming again and found myself holding someone's hands and jumping into the air. I wanted to try flying.

I grabbed his hands and jumped in the air, flapping my arms like a bird. I went up toward the ceiling and started hovering. It took a lot of effort and wasn't very effective. Again, the experience was very short, even though I put in great effort.

I decided that was not a good technique either.

In the dream, there was a third scene where I was walking toward the top of a hill. I thought, *Why don't I do a spiritual exercise and call on the Mahanta?* I had read somewhere that when you have a Soul Travel experience there is always a Master nearby, so you can chant a spiritual word (like HU) and ask for help. When I asked, I had always gotten help from the Inner Master, the Mahanta.

This time it didn't work as planned. I was stunned!

Then I realized why. I had put in the least effort. I was calling on the Mahanta to do it for me instead of teaching me how to do it myself. Of course, this was just my lesson for that time; for others it's different.

By then I was nearing the top of the hill. When I reached the top, I realized I was supposed to take responsibility for this experience.

On the way down the hill, I found myself in a big city with cars, buildings, and people.

Then I followed an inner nudge, Why not try it with focus?

In the dream I thought, *Why don't I do a spiritual exercise and call on the Mahanta?*

I would focus my attention to a pinpoint and move myself there in my Soul body. I decided to focus on a bright yellow flyer on the other side of the street. I started walking toward it and kept my attention focused. But I reached the advertisement without results. I needed another focus point. I had to look for something not too close, but still close enough to stay focused on it.

I realized that just like in life, I have to set goals—including my spiritual goals—and make them reasonable. I decided flying is just a sensation. My real goal was to find out how to be fully aware as Soul.

I chose another object and was walking toward it. Then when I was halfway to it, thinking of goals, I woke up because the purpose of my experience was fulfilled.

I knew then that I didn't have to put so much effort into Soul Travel, only focus. This is what the Mahanta was trying to teach me. The mind is easily distracted, so it needs a lot of practice and self-discipline. The outcome is a consciousness which is always aware of what is going on.

When I notice some other thought flooding in or throwing my focus off, I put that thought on the edge of my vision. I just move it to the side so I'm not distracted.

My goal is to reach full consciousness in whatever I'm doing as Soul. I practice keeping my focus, my awareness, during the whole day, not just during Soul Travel or my spiritual exercises. I try to be fully in the present.

Would you like to have a lucid dream? Try this next exercise from *Past Lives, Dreams, and Soul Travel*

> I decided flying is just a sensation. My real goal was to find out how to be fully aware as Soul.

by Harold Klemp.[3] Harold Klemp is also the Dream Master, who will work with anyone who asks. He will not interfere with anyone but can guide and protect if asked. He works with people of all religions and beliefs throughout the world.

Soul Travel Exercise:

To Dream in Full Consciousness

Do you want to learn how to move in full consciousness to a new or higher plane during the dream state? Then try this technique.

Before sleep, place your attention on the Living ECK Master's face. Now try to keep his face in mind as you doze off. Then await his coming as the Dream Master.

In dreamland, anchor your attention on some solid object in the room, like a chair, a clock, etc. Hold that image in mind. Then give yourself a thought command.

Say, *I am awake in this dream.*

Let your attention fix on the solid object chosen as a point of reference above. Feel yourself begin to rise. Layers of clouds like soft cotton puffs will drift past. Thus you shift into a new state of consciousness every bit as real as this physical one.

A shift to a new state of consciousness is a shift to a new plane.

If it's hard to keep your attention on the solid object in your dream, don't worry about

---

You shift into a new state of consciousness every bit as real as this physical one.

it. You will sink into the dream state and later awaken in the usual way.

Another technique to dream in full consciousness is to take the role of a silent witness. Watch others play out their roles, much as you would watch a movie.

Other techniques to try are to start and stop a dream. Or make it more bright or dim. For fun, switch from black and white to color.

Try things.

Still another way to dream in full consciousness is to watch yourself drop off to sleep. Catch the moment of slipping into the dream state.

It does take practice, but it can be restful to your body while doing these exercises of switching into a higher state of consciousness. There need be no trace of fear. You can also rise from one dream level to a higher one, in full consciousness.

A question comes up: What to do if you are in a conscious dream and want to return to your body?

Just feel yourself back in it. That's all there is to it. You will return in an instant.

A question comes up: What to do if you are in a conscious dream and want to return to your body?

THE FUTURE REVEALED IN SOUL TRAVEL

Some very special dream-travel experiences led Sheila to an awareness of her husband-to-be:

 everal years ago I started having dreams of a man I'd never met. I had been feeling really lonely before that, but suddenly I felt I was not alone anymore. I became aware of this particular Soul who I knew would be in my future. I had several dreams where I spoke with him on the phone. There was a great feeling of warmth and familiarity. It was very powerful. I felt I was no longer alone but in an established relationship.

Someone mentioned a name (we'll call him Ted), and as soon as they mentioned it, I recognized the name. I knew this was the man I had been aware of in my dreams. Even though we'd never met or spoken, there was inner communication between us, as Soul, for about three months.

Then one day when I was staying with my stepfather, who also happened to be Ted's friend, my life changed forever. I happened to pick up the phone that day when Ted called, and I heard his voice for the first time. I knew it was *him*— the love of my life! I became aware that we had a prior agreement to be together in this life and help each other unfold spiritually.

I soon discovered that before we met, he'd also had a dream with me! Ted didn't know it was me until we spoke on the phone. The Mahanta, his inner spiritual guide, had brought Ted to a place in the inner worlds where he was introduced to a woman he knew he would be with. By the way, I recognized the Mahanta as my guide, too, once I found out about him!

I moved to where Ted lived, without ever having actually met him, and we've been together ever since. When we connected in the physical world, we had already been relating Soul-to-Soul on the inner planes for a long time.

> I knew this was the man I had been aware of in my dreams. Even though we'd never met or spoken, there was inner communication between us.

When we were finally together in the physical world, it was like meeting an old friend, someone I had always known. It doesn't mean we don't have the trials and challenges that other couples have, but we have the awareness of a commitment beyond just a physical relationship. We are also together to help each other grow spiritually. Helping each other along on the spiritual path is what keeps us together and growing as a couple.

Prophetic dreams may also involve Soul Travel. We may experience something on a higher plane, so that we don't feel such a shock when it happens here on earth. Victor had this experience:

Prophetic dreams may also involve Soul Travel. We may experience something on a higher plane, so that we don't feel such a shock when it happens here on earth.

I felt like I had been going backward in my spiritual unfoldment. It seemed nothing was working like it should, like it used to. Was I being tested and failing over and over again?

My life seemed a mess. I had moved twice in one year, couldn't seem to earn a living, my health went from bad to worse, and I had gotten a divorce. Usually, I stayed positive through it all, but one day I hit bottom.

I actually had had a dream that warned me about this.

In the dream I was at a huge amusement park similar to Disneyland, with many unusual rides. One of them had no line at all, and my inner spiritual teacher, the Mahanta, told me to go to that ride. On the door it said Ground Zero. This was about one month before events of September 11, 2001, flooded the news media with that phrase.

I opened the door and saw a chasm of such depth, I couldn't even see the bottom. I thought, *No way!* Then I saw a stairway and said to the Mahanta, "I'll take the stairs, if that's OK!" So I did, and it took me quite a while. I woke up from the dream feeling I had barely escaped an extreme experience.

Life kept getting tougher in some ways and easier in others. Still, the tough days did me in. The day I hit bottom, I had the toughest time. I knew I had fulfilled the "ride" I was supposed to take, just like in my dream.

That night, I had another dream:

I was doing some task for the Mahanta, and afterward he kissed me on one cheek, then the other, in thanks. I was almost moved to tears, there was so much love and appreciation in it. I felt like I could go through anything for that love.

Soul can move through time as well as space. Mimi's pro- phetic dream shows this.

So Soul can move through time as well as space. Mimi's prophetic dream shows this phenomenon even more clearly:

One time I was house-sitting where there was a cat. I let the cat go outside in the morning, and it never came back that day. It was a really hot day, and I was worried about him. That night I went to bed, concerned about the cat.

I had a dream that the cat came back in the morning. In the dream I went to the back door and opened it, and he walked in. It was still dark outside. I didn't even know the cat was at the door; I just thought he'd be there when I opened it. That was the end of the dream.

In the morning I opened my eyes, stood up, and walked to the back door. I opened the door, and there was the cat—just like a replay of the dream! It was even still dark outside, just like in my dream.

Everyday Soul Travel Adventures

Even when wide awake, we can have a Soul Travel experience, simply by staying aware and watching the signs from God. That's what Laura did:

I was thinking of ending a relationship that was not really going anywhere. My boyfriend, Joe, said he loved me and didn't want to lose me, but he didn't want to marry me either. I decided to break up with him, but he couldn't accept it and kept calling me.

Then I had a series of dreams that guided me to move, and I did. However, Joe showed up in the city I moved to and continued calling me. I still loved him and didn't know what to do, or even what I wanted. So I asked the Inner Master, the Mahanta, what to do.

I asked for help with this question every night for three nights, but I didn't remember my dreams. I was too distraught to get a clear answer. I wanted to be with Joe, but I suspected it was not a good idea.

One day I got caught in a traffic jam. I was at the end of my rope. Sitting in my car, I yelled, "Mahanta, what am I going to do?"

At that moment I saw the car's license plate in front of me. It said No Joe. It was so clear. I felt like I was out of my body in that moment, knowing, as Soul, exactly what was right and

Even when wide awake, we can have a Soul Travel experience, simply by staying aware and watching the signs from God.

what I had to do. The next time Joe called, I was able to say no, and that was the end of that.

Sometimes you can be in the middle of an experience and not see it. This waking dream really helped me. I saw the whole picture from Soul's point of view. God's love is such a major part of every waking and sleeping moment. We just have to notice it!

OUT-OF-BODY EXPERIENCES

Helga found freedom in the simplicity of leaving her physical body and letting herself soar:

> I was in the Swiss Alps, a student at a body-work seminar. Lying on a massage table, I was very relaxed after some great bodywork. Suddenly my consciousness expanded, and I saw mountains and sky. I was in the middle and could see all around, all at once. I was pure Soul with no limits!
>
> I felt my consciousness expanding more and more. It was very special. I realized I was not on the same plane as my physical body. Someone was still working on my body, but I was somewhere else.
>
> That was such a wonderful, special experience, and I so wanted to have it again. A few months later I found Eckankar, which taught me how to do that.
>
> My desire as Soul was to have this experience of spiritual freedom. I know something is God's will when I am given these experiences as beautiful gifts to help me understand who I am and what I really want as Soul.

Classic out-of-body Soul Travel experiences can

Suddenly my consciousness expanded, and I saw mountains and sky. I was in the middle and could see all around, all at once.

happen as people are preparing to find the Light and Sound of God. Carl's experience got him started in his search for truth and spiritual freedom:

> *O*ne of the first experiences I ever had with Soul Travel was a clear transition between dream travel and classic out-of-body travel.
>
> I had dozed off to sleep and instantaneously was out of bed and in my living room. There was a great feeling of freedom and exhilaration. But I couldn't indulge it because of a danger.
>
> A certain negative entity walked through my living-room door. I felt shock and fear, which made the feeling of freedom lessen. I stood for a moment. Then an angel appeared and told me clearly and concisely to walk directly toward the entity and tell it, "In the name of God, leave my space!"
>
> As I approached the entity, I did this. The entity vanished, poof! I was back in bed immediately. I felt that the "angel" who helped me was a divine personage. I thought at first maybe it was God, but I didn't think God would talk to just me. I felt there must be some intermediary. (Now I know it was the Mahanta, my inner spiritual teacher and guide.) This feeling led me to be a spiritual seeker. This experience also helped me let go of a lot of fears, especially the fear of death.
>
> Not long after this, I found Eckankar. I learned about psychic space and that nothing can invade my space unless I allow it. I learned that I can confront my fear, knowing I have the Mahanta's protection. And I learned that I am more than just a body; I am Soul.

I learned that I am more than just a body; I am Soul.

CURIOSITY TO SOUL TRAVEL

Robert had an experience that began with a desire and ended in a classic out-of-body Soul Travel experience:

I was sitting on a porch by a river in West Virginia. Across the river were some small, forested mountains. I looked at one I especially liked with a tall tree on top. I spoke inwardly with the Mahanta, saying, "According to you, I can project myself to that tree up there and look back at myself." So I tried it.

I looked at the tree and concentrated on the tree, being there, and imagined looking at my body. Instantly I was out of my body, and I saw myself! I'd never felt such freedom! I was so excited I popped right back into my body. Later, after much practice and experimentation, I learned that if I got too emotionally high, not staying balanced, I would return abruptly to my body. I learned this is a key to success in every endeavor—a balanced emotional or mental state.

Some people just want to experience Soul Travel one time as a means to prove to themselves that they can really separate from the body. Suzanne was one:

I asked myself, "Was it really Soul Travel?"

*A*fter a lovely day, I was lying in bed, wondering about Soul Travel. I wanted to prove to myself that Soul Travel was real, that the teachings of Eckankar were real. I thought I had Soul Traveled but wasn't sure. I asked myself, "Was it really Soul Travel?"

As I lay there, I sang HU. I relaxed com-

pletely into the sound of HU. I discovered later
that the relaxation was very important. I felt my
life force start to withdraw up my body, very
slowly, very softly and gently. There was no fear.
I was aware that my life force was really me.

Then I started paying attention to the process. My attention was moving up to my Spiritual Eye, called the Tisra Til in Eckankar. Located
between and just slightly above the eyebrows,
this is where we also see with our inner vision
into the spiritual worlds.

I heard a pop, like a cork out of a bottle. I
was immediately out of my body—over my
house—such freedom and joy!

I was so elated, filled with gratitude, great
love and light. This had all been done so gently,
with such great care. My spiritual guide, the
Mahanta, was with me, saying, "See, I am who
I say I am, and you are who you are. I know who
you are."

Then I heard a choir—beautiful high voices.
My whole being was resonating with the Sound
of God. There was a very strong light. I couldn't
see the choir singing, but I heard them very
clearly.

Next, I visited a Golden Wisdom Temple,
and the Mahanta was giving a discourse, or
lesson. This all happened very quickly.

Being separated from the body with no fear
helped me see that, as Soul, I would survive
beyond the death of my physical body.

Suzanne also learned the power of wonder. Simply
wondering, or being curious, can help us move out of
our physical awareness into Soul Travel, as she did.

Being sepa-
rated from the
body with no
fear helped me
see that, as
Soul, I would
survive beyond
the death of my
physical body.

More often, Soul Travel can be very subtle. Sometimes people are unaware they are even going anywhere until someone validates the experience, as in Carmen's case:

More often, Soul Travel can be very subtle.

I had a Soul Travel experience after I met someone with whom I instantly fell in love. He was a cabin steward on a cruise ship. It seemed the feeling was mutual, but he was not allowed to fraternize with the passengers. Nonetheless, we spent a little time together off the ship, with him as tour guide. When I arrived home, I felt like I was connected with him inwardly. Since there was no ship-to-shore phone service at that time, we could never talk when he was on the ship. Yet the inner communication seemed to be much stronger. I wrote him letters telling him what I felt and sensed. In a dream I had seen him in a hospital bed. Next he was smoking with a group of friends. Then he threw his cigarettes away.

Later, when I visited him briefly in Hawaii, I told him I felt very connected, and he said, "Oh yes, we have been. I have been with you, and I am with you." He told me he had indeed been in the hospital and later had been under a lot of stress and had started smoking, but quit a few days later. I feel we've been friends for many lifetimes, and the love we share, as Soul, created a bond of love so strong that we could communicate without words or modern technology.

I felt a tremendous surge of God's love in this experience. I know there were many lessons in it for me.

Just a note about inner communication or Soul

Travel to meet someone else: it is an important spiritual law not to invade another's space or privacy. Often an encounter happens because there is an agreement from Soul to Soul.

Sometimes we are resolving karma when we communicate with someone inwardly. We are learning our spiritual lessons as God's love helps us lighten our karmic load and gain more spiritual freedom. As Harold Klemp puts it:

> *Spiritual freedom is growing into a state of more godliness. Becoming more aware of the presence of God. How do you do this? By becoming aware of the lessons behind your everyday experiences. This is how you grow into a loving awareness of the presence of God.*[4]

DUAL CONSCIOUSNESS AS SOUL TRAVEL

Morgan had an experience where she was out of her body and experienced God's love:

At an ECK Worship Service I was listening to a member of our clergy lead us through a spiritual exercise. The exercise was based on the theme "The Light and Sound of God." I was happily filled with a feeling of total peace and love, the kind that can only be from a divine source, Holy Spirit.

I let myself bask in this love while I listened, but I could no longer hear the speaker's words. I suddenly found myself moving upward into a column of pure white light. It wasn't like any light I've ever seen; it had a shiny or shimmering quality to it. It's so hard to describe in words!

It is an important spiritual law not to invade another's space or privacy. Often an encounter happens because there is an agreement from Soul to Soul.

It had a life of its own, pulling me upward into the higher levels of heaven, or so it seemed.

It was all so quick and so subtle that I nearly discounted the experience until I could hear the speaker talking again, telling us about where we could go and what to look for on the inner planes during the spiritual exercise. This brought me right back.

I was grateful to see the contrast of where I'd been and then coming back to being conscious of my body and mind. Now I knew I had definitely had a Soul Travel experience, no matter how brief or how gentle. God's love was surrounding me and holding me for a precious moment in time which I am sure I will never forget.

Would you like to focus your attention on having a Soul Travel experience? Try this next exercise every night, for one month. It is from Harold Klemp's book *ECK Masters and You: An Illustrated Guide*[5]:

Soul Travel Exercise: The Easy Way

Just before sleep, place attention upon your Spiritual Eye. It is between the eyebrows. Then sing HU or God silently.

Just before sleep, place attention upon your Spiritual Eye. It is between the eyebrows. Then sing HU or God silently.

Fix attention on a blank movie screen in your inner vision, and keep it free of any pictures. If unwanted mental thoughts, images, or pictures do flash up on the screen of your imagination, replace them with the face of the Living ECK Master.

After a few minutes of silence, you may

hear a faint clicking sound in one ear, perhaps like the sound of a cork popping from a bottle. You will find yourself in the Soul form in a most natural way, looking back at your physical body in bed.

Now, would you like to go on a short outing?

There is nothing to fear, for no harm can come to you while outside the body. The Mahanta will be with you to keep watch over your progress and offer support. After a while, the Soul body will return and slide gently into the physical self.

That is all there is to it.

If this exercise is not successful the first time, try it again later. The technique works. It has worked for many others.

> You will find yourself in the Soul form in a most natural way, looking back at your physical body in bed.

Thomas had this experience, and it showed him the reality of Soul Travel:

I was sitting and contemplating, doing a spiritual exercise, when I began to hear these sounds. First thunder, then running water, the buzzing of bees, and finally the music of a flute. I was immediately jolted back into my body and asked, "What's this?" I don't think I realized I had been out of my body until I abruptly came back!

On a chart that Eckankar has of the various levels of heaven, these are all sounds from several planes going from the Physical Plane (thunder) to the Mental Plane (running water), Etheric Plane (buzzing of bees), and the Soul Plane (flute).

I realized later, after looking at this chart

and remembering what I had heard, that I'd had
a very quick Soul Travel experience. I realized
the key for me was gratitude. I had been feeling
very good about my life and grateful for it. Also,
the sense of freedom helped.

Are you ready for more adventure? Turn the page
to learn about the connection between Soul Travel
and past lives.

5

Soul Travel and Past Lives

It's a little hard to understand, but Soul is not a two- or three-dimensional being. Soul is multidimensional. It shares all the aspects of God. Soul can be everywhere at all times, and all places at the same time. This is that part of God that you are.

— Harold Klemp, *The Slow Burning Love of God*, Mahanta Transcripts, Book 13[1]

---

eincarnation is a belief common to many religions of the world. The Bible appears to refer to it briefly in Luke 9, regarding one of the old prophets as having "risen" again.[2]

But you don't have to believe anyone else. Prove it to yourself with some of the Soul Travel exercises you'll find in this chapter.

SOUL TRAVEL TO VIEW THE PAST

Discovering your past can help you heal old wounds and bring love and understanding to difficult situations. Rita found just such a healing with a past-life discovery:

Discovering your past can help you heal old wounds and bring love and understanding to difficult situations.

*M*y whole life I have dealt with an inferiority complex. I decided to do a spiritual exercise to find out more.

*M*y whole life I have dealt with an inferiority complex. The cause revealed itself over time and through several incidents.

Ever since I can remember, I've had a certain discomfort with Southern accents I'd hear in movies or on television. For some reason they gave me the creeps. But I never actually met anyone with a Southern drawl until my adult years.

One of my coworkers, Gerry, had this type of accent, and for me it was like hearing fingernails on a blackboard. I'd never had trouble with any of my coworkers before, but I had lots of issues with Gerry. We had an incredibly hard time working together.

I decided to do a spiritual exercise to find out more. The Mahanta, my inner spiritual guide, helped me move from my emotional body to a higher viewpoint as Soul. I could see the anger in my emotional body from this higher consciousness, then I would be pulled back into the emotion. This happened five or six times. Then I fell asleep and woke up in a dream.

In the dream, I was conscious of everything. I was an African-American in the Deep South, walking through a grove of trees. It was in the early twentieth century. The trees were hung with Spanish moss. It was dark, gray, and damp there. I had a horrible feeling about the place. Then I saw why. There were black men hanging from trees all around. I felt fear, anger, rage, and profound grief. These men had been lynched.

I woke up from the dream with a terrible pain in my neck. But a healing had begun. It took about a year to resolve everything. I realized my coworker, Gerry, had reminded me of that horrible time in my past life, due to his Southern drawl. My relationship with him improved and eventually healed. The change was amazing.

I understood from that experience why I'd always had feelings of inferiority and walked into a room with my head down. Now I know who I really am—Soul, beyond the realm of race, creed, or skin color.

As we'll see in the following story, Kelly had had dream-travel experiences from the time she was very young, but she didn't know it until she discovered Soul Travel. Her recurring dreams helped her uncover a past life that would help her let go of old limitations:

My problem-solving techniques often have two parts to them. Part one is kicking and screaming. Part two is surrender to the Holy Spirit.

In the first part of this problem I was feeling trapped in my life. I felt like I couldn't breathe. I couldn't really be myself or express myself. At this time in my life I was having two recurring dreams.

One recurring dream I'd had from the time I was twelve years old. I was underwater and would wake up gasping for air. The last time I had the dream, my inner guide, the Mahanta, said clearly, "It's all right; you can breathe." I took a big gulp, and it was air, not water!

When I was young, my brother and I had been captivated by the story of the *Titanic*. We read everything we could about it. After that, I

> I understood why I'd always walked into a room with my head down. Now I know who I really am—Soul, beyond the realm of race, creed, or skin color.

thought no more of it for years. Then, many years later, I started having negative thoughts about myself. I began thinking things like, "I just can't get it right. I can't be perfect enough."

That's when I had a series of dreams where I was in a place that looked like a gigantic warehouse. The men inside were building a huge, magnificent ship. I was an engineer on the project, and I *knew* there was something wrong with it. But I did not follow through with my responsibility. I let someone else tell me what to do, when I knew I should follow my heart!

In my dream, I was responsible for providing materials to make fully walled compartments, but I was persuaded to save money and make them only partially walled. The partially walled compartments compromised the ship's ability to survive hull damage. I feel that the money saved was used for shows of opulence and glitz.

For a long time I still struggled with my feelings of not being good enough. I felt like I couldn't handle responsibility. My mind wanted to worry and mentalize over my past mistakes. Finally I learned the way to face myself is by singing HU. This helped me "switch channels," or shift consciousness to the higher viewpoint of Soul, to where I can do the most good today.

Now when I do my spiritual exercises, I think of the mind as a puppy when it tries to pull me back. It's just a puppy playing, so I just let it play—and leave the past in the past.

Kelly discovered the power of HU. Singing HU with love (as explained on page 98) is the simplest, most direct way to shift to a higher viewpoint, way

For a long time I struggled with past mistakes. Finally I learned to face myself by singing HU.

above your earthly troubles. Singing HU for twenty minutes a day is one of the best spiritual exercises you can do.

Soul Travel Insights and Time Travel

Wynona found her spiritual exercises to be a saving grace, giving her insights into a past life affecting her present one:

I met a fellow musician who was an expert guitarist. Matt and I became close buddies very quickly. There was a lot of love between us—so much that it felt uncomfortable, since he was married. I felt so drawn to him, I didn't know what to think of it.

Later I felt an inner urging to visit the Southwest, where he lived. This would be partly a vacation for me and partly a musical performance with Matt. I stayed with him and his family, who knew we were just friends but also saw we were closely connected. When I left, he and I both cried. His wife seemed to understand, comforting Matt in his sorrow.

During the drive home, I had to pull over and cry again. I began to consider moving to where he lived to perform with him musically. But would that be wise?

When I arrived home, I did a spiritual exercise to ask my inner guide, the Mahanta, if there was a past-life connection between me and Matt and, if so, what to do about it.

In a Soul Travel experience, I was shown a brief scene from ancient Egypt. I was a man in that life—a priest—and I was visiting a woman

Singing HU with love is the simplest, most direct way to shift to a higher viewpoint, way above your earthly troubles.

in jail. It was Matt in that former life. The woman had misused her power somehow. I broke her out of jail because I loved her very much. The scene faded, and I came out of my contemplation.

The next step was to check out job possibilities in the Southwest, where Matt lived, but nothing worked out and it just didn't feel right. I backed off of moving there.

Several months later I was viewing another fragment of that life in Egypt:

We were in the desert, trying to escape in chariots. Soldiers were chasing us. One caught up with us and speared her. She lay dying on the sand, and I couldn't save her. As I knelt over her, I took a spear through the back myself. (I'll note here that I had back problems in this present life at the time of these recalls.)

I did another spiritual exercise, and the Mahanta showed me that in this life Matt wanted me to help him again, by breaking him out of his marriage. He wanted more creative freedom. But by helping him again, I would be held back spiritually, and hold him back as well. The lesson this time was to meet the same situation and not do the same thing. I stepped away. As it turned out, his marriage did break up anyway. I had no idea this was happening at the time I was drawn to him.

Once I had learned the spiritual lesson, I was no longer attracted to him. The heartbreak went away, and that cycle ended.

To explore past lives that may be affecting this one, try the next exercise. Also, there are many more

In this life the lesson was to meet the same situation and not do the same thing.

past-life exploration exercises in my book *Exploring Past Lives to Heal the Present.*

Soul Travel Exercise: Soul Travel and Time

1. When you find yourself in a situation that is uncomfortable for no apparent reason, consider that the discomfort might stem from a past life. Write or think of a phrase that relates to your discomfort. For example, "I feel fearful around my boss." Or "I feel my wife treats me like a child." This will help you get in better touch with the situation.

2. Ask the Mahanta to take you directly to the pertinent past-life record. Chant the word *mana*, which is the word to lift you, Soul, to the Causal Plane, where images of past lives are stored.

3. Trust the images that come to you, and write them down so you can look at them later as more insights come. You might get validation in some way, and eventually the old images may pass off, healing the wound.

Ask the Mahanta to take you directly to the pertinent past-life record. Trust the images that come to you.

LETTING GO OF THE PAST

Past-life exploration may take a little more persistence and detective work than you expect. I've noticed that it's often hard to remember some of the important details or more traumatic lifetimes because they are so disturbing. Henry was tenacious in looking for an answer to his insomnia:

As Soul I have a 360-degree awareness, like rising above the clouds and seeing clearly in all directions, only more so.

*T*o me, there's a very thin veil between this life and past lives. I see Soul Travel is not really travel, but lifting a veil between worlds. As Soul I have a 360-degree awareness, like rising above the clouds and seeing clearly in all directions, only more so.

I see a continuity of life—past, present, and future. The key to being in Soul awareness is love. I can shift into that awareness at any moment. Looking at past lives to see where some problems began, allows me to see the root causes of those problems.

From the time I was a little boy, I'd had trouble sleeping. As an adult, I was trying to fall asleep one night. I asked the Mahanta, my inner spiritual teacher, "Why do I have trouble sleeping?"

I suddenly saw myself as a woman in the early 1700s in London, in a large, beautiful home. I was overwhelmed by a very sad, tragic feeling. I was afraid to sleep, because everyone who went to sleep wasn't waking up! They had malaria. It was very hot and humid. I knew if I went to sleep, I would die.

So in this life I still have a fear of going to sleep. For a long time I had insomnia. Part of it was healed by remembering that past life. Now I can sleep most nights, but if there's noise, I still have a difficult time sleeping. I was still missing a piece of the puzzle.

Then one morning I was making breakfast after a sleepless night. I asked the Mahanta, "Why am I so sensitive to noise?" Standing right there at the sink, I shifted into a higher state of consciousness.

I saw another lifetime, this one in World War II. Because there was a war going on, my family and I had to be on constant alert. We were constantly bombarded with the sounds of planes, bombs, and people screaming. Also, being Jewish, we had to always be in hiding. My senses were very attuned to sound, because it kept me alive. For that period of time, it affected my sleep patterns. I died in that war.

Consequently, noise or any kind of distraction during the night—even distant noises—subconsciously reminded me of that lifetime and jarred my nerves. Unless it was completely quiet, I felt a nervous tension and couldn't go to sleep.

I got my answer by just asking the question! Once I ask a question, I simply shift into the awareness of knowing I am Soul, and from that vantage point it's like being at the top of a mountain. I can see everything I need to see from a higher perspective. It feels more detached, like I'm stepping back. I let the images come to me. It's not just the images, but also the emotions from the past life.

PHYSICAL HEALING FROM PAST-LIFE EXPLORATION

Healing from past lives can lead to a physical healing in this life, as we let go of the old fear we carry from the old life into this one. This was the case with me.

For years I've had pain or sensitivity in my back just below my right shoulder blade. It was always sensitive to touch. I wanted to jump out of my skin every time someone touched me

Healing from past lives can lead to a physical healing in this life, as we let go of the old fear we carry from the old life into this one.

there, even for a massage. A related issue for me was that I had mostly mistrusted men I loved.

I contemplated on this as I did a spiritual exercise, but got no clear direction. However, I began to feel sad for no apparent reason. I even started crying, then stopped myself to ask, "Why?"

Later, I was lying on the floor after exercising, completely relaxed, but my shoulder still hurt. Because I was so relaxed, I felt as if I was apart from my body. Again the sadness came, but this time I was separate from it, from my body consciousness. Since I knew I was out of my body, I knew I could travel back and forth on the Time Track. I could check out the past-life connection!

I moved into an image of someone being stabbed in the back. It was me. I'd known this was a possibility, but I had no idea who had stabbed me. I was shocked to see that it was my husband, who I thought loved and cherished me! As I left that life, I realized that he had only married me for my money. He was really in love with someone else, whom he proceeded to marry once I was out of the way by his hand.

After that realization I did another spiritual exercise, this time to heal the pain. I'll share it with you here.

Think of any lasting, painful images that may be from this life or a past life. Look at how the situation may have resulted from old karma.

Soul Travel Exercise: Healing with Love

1. Think of any lasting, painful images that may be from this life or a past life. Look at how the situation may have resulted from old karma or from being in a limiting attitude or viewpoint.

Finally, consider how you (or someone else) may have caused the situation in another lifetime.

2. Forgive yourself for any misdeeds. Forgive the offending party for meting out your karma.

3. Imagine the most beautiful ocean you can, sparkling and singing with the Light and Sound of God. Imagine this is the Ocean of Love and Mercy, or the essence of God. Throw all the images from your painful past into the Ocean of Love and Mercy and watch them dissolve into love. You can now let them go.

After I do this exercise, I feel so much lighter and freer. The key for me is in truly forgiving everyone involved, including myself.

SOUL PLAYS MANY ROLES

Forgiveness works best for me if I can find the lifetime where I was the offending party, or the perpetrator. The next experience I had shows a more complete cycle of lifetimes:

A deep sadness came over me again. I had more layers of grief to peel away, but where did they come from? I decided to do another spiritual exercise to find out exactly what I needed to heal. I saw myself as a baby in this life, and some familiar but forgotten images appeared.

In this lifetime, when I was a baby, my mother was very depressed. She had the tendency to

Forgiveness works best for me if I can find the lifetime where I was the offending party, or the perpetrator.

ignore us children—not feed us, hold us, or comfort us. I knew this only because my sister was much older and remembers it all. I was only three months old when my mother was taken away and put in a mental institution.

But I saw some images my sister never told me about, because she had never seen these things occur. My mother grabbed my leg and pulled hard (I've had hip problems all this life) to get me in the right position to change my diapers. She was rough and unthinking, unable to hear my cries of pain. She was angry and hit me when I cried.

Since we have earned everything we experience, I knew I had to look further, into a lifetime where I had earned this treatment. I did so and saw an image of a woman who was yelling at her children, whom she made work to help support her and a new baby. The baby was in her arms, but it was as if she didn't know or care about it. The woman was me. I was an unfeeling mother, and I cared mainly about survival, though my children needed love, attention, and caring. Love was a secondary concern, if any at all. I looked for ways to escape my fate, having been married to a drunk whom I kicked out. I had married him to escape an abusive, alcoholic father.

In that life I wormed my way into higher society and found a man who would marry me and take care of me but not my children. I sent money home to the oldest one, who took care of all the rest.

The karma came back to me in this life as my older sister took care of us most of the time,

> Since we have earned everything we experience, I knew I had to look further, into a lifetime where I had earned this treatment.

while we lived with my grandparents. Then my father came back and sent us to foster homes, promising he'd marry someone to bring us back together as a family again. He married, but his new wife didn't want children. The events of the past came full circle.

ASK GOD FOR HELP

Relationship issues are a hotbed of past-life karma. It often seems a mystery until we ask God for help, as Jacob did:

    noticed a pattern in my life. I could watch certain people do something mean, and I would overlook it because that person was so important to me.

I had a girlfriend like that at the time. I recognized this was not a good way for me to live. While lying in bed one night, I asked God to show me why I attracted this sort of person.

I saw an image of a past life where one brother killed another and I said nothing, to protect my status. Then I saw another life where my sister was abusing a child and I still didn't say anything. A third life appeared in which I was the abuser.

When I became aware of all this, I was awake in my bed. I was watching these scenes all at once, through a series of tunnels, like watching three different movie screens. I could see these were three of my lifetimes. Then they all fell together and I felt they were all a part of me. It felt like all the bodies from those lives slammed together, and I woke up, back to my body. I had been out of my body, watching these scenes, and

Relationship issues are a hotbed of past-life karma. It often seems a mystery until we ask God for help.

yet I could still see all around my room.

When I was back in my body, I knew that I could change, that it was my choice. I decided I didn't want to be that way anymore. I didn't want to stand by while someone was unkind or cruel to others. My relationships with these kinds of people changed, and I ended my romantic relationship as well.

The most primary relationship is with ourselves. I've studied, written, and taught the subject, because I feel it is so important. I realize more and more how vital it is to love myself before others can love me, or before I can truly love others. Here's what happened as I worked on loving myself.

When I was back in my body, I knew that I could change, that it was my choice. I decided I didn't want to be that way anymore.

I found there were many layers of emotions I had buried deep inside me. The more I gave myself love, the more the sadness and anger had to be pushed out. I wondered how I could handle it!

Inwardly I asked for help from the Mahanta and received guidance. I got a few ideas to use that helped me get through that difficult time without too many other people having to experience my negative emotions. Here is the exercise I used:

Soul Travel Exercise:

Breathing In God's Love

1. Take a few deep breaths, relaxing as much as possible. Sing HU, the ancient love song to God (explained on page 13) several times, while

imagining all the love you have felt in your life building into a big ball of love that warms your heart.

2. Imagine sending all of this love to God.

3. If you still feel anger buried within you, sing HU a few more times. Imagine the anger surfacing and passing off like steam. When I did this part myself, I imagined the steam turning into little hearts. The next part came as a surprise to me.

4. Breathe in God's love, accepting the love, the fullness of God's love coming back to you. Welcome it into the painful areas of yourself or your life to help them heal. Be a babe in the arms of God, knowing you are cherished, loved, and protected, always.

Children are such good examples of accepting love as well as the mysteries of God. Many children remember past lives when they are very little, about three or four years old, but Michael remembered as a teen:

> *W*hen I was a teenager, I remember having an almost direct knowledge that there were past lives. I had a dream that I remembered very clearly.
>
> I was in a room looking at four different men. One was Hindu, wearing a white sheet around him like Gandhi wore. One was Chinese, and the other two were French or English. I knew that all of these men were me in some of

Many children remember past lives when they are very little, but Michael remembered as a teen.

A Soul Travel
experience
helped me to
know what I
would experi-
ence spiritually
as an adult and
also prepared
me for the
reality of life
beyond the
physical world.

my former lives. I knew without any doubt, because I was awake in the dream, very conscious of it. It was a very real experience.

I can tell it was a Soul Travel experience because my viewpoint was not like a physical perspective. We were in a transparent room, and I was viewing it from somewhere up on the ceiling! At the same time, I could connect with all these individuals. I felt what these people were feeling, even though I was on the outside. I was like an actor who knows how the scene is supposed to be played. It was like observing myself acting on a stage.

This helped me to know what I would experience spiritually as an adult and also prepared me for the reality of life beyond the physical world.

Children have so much to share with us about the reality of the heavenly worlds. The next chapter offers just a small part of their wisdom and experience.

6

Young Soul Travel Experts

Children have the wisdom of God and are closer to it than many people who have spent years in this world gaining all kinds of knowledge about the nature of religion. Children have it naturally.

— Harold Klemp, *The Secret of Love*, Mahanta Transcripts, Book 14[1]

Children have the wisdom of God naturally.

As very young children, we may hear nursery rhymes that suggest or describe Soul Travel. For example, *Wynken, Blynken, and Nod*, by Eugene Field.[2] Part of the poem says:

"Wynken, Blynken, and Nod one night
Sailed off in a wooden shoe,—
. . . .
'Twas all so pretty a sail, it seemed
As if it could not be;
And some folks thought 'twas a dream they'd
dreamed
Of sailing that beautiful sea;
But I shall name you the fisherman three:
Wynken,
Blynken,
And Nod.

Wynken and Blynken are two little eyes,
And Nod is a little head,
And the wooden shoe that sailed the skies
Is a wee one's trundle-bed;
So shut your eyes while Mother sings
Of wonderful sights that be,
And you shall see the beautiful things
As you rock on the misty sea.

YOUTHFUL JOURNEYS OUT OF THE BODY

Soul Travel happens at any age, and perhaps more easily with youth.

Soul Travel happens at any age, and perhaps more easily with youth. They are so happy to imagine, create, and make believe. These are all aspects of Soul's divine gift of imagination that can take us into the heavenly worlds. Youth are experts at this, though they may not remember when they get older. Luckily, Sheila did. Instead of a wooden shoe, like Wynken, Blynken, and Nod, Sheila had much more modern vehicles in her dreams:

I used to have a variety of dreams relating to flying cars. They flew through the air above the ground, like in the *Star Wars* movie "The Phantom Menace." Sometimes it felt good. But sometimes it was scary, when I was escaping enemies. I felt it was real because it was so vivid. They were true adventures.

Kari, who is now in high school, says she loved to Soul Travel as a child. She found it helped her live her life better by the time she became a teenager:

When I was little I had dreams where I would fly around the living room. My parents were there, sitting on the couch, and I would fly above them. There was a balcony, and I would fly off the railing, but they wouldn't see me. I wasn't scared, I was happy. I remember only positive feelings. At the time, I thought I was dreaming, but now I know it was Soul Travel.

More recently, in eighth grade, I was having trouble with my identity. I was acting differently than who I really was. I had a dream where I was sitting on a bench in a Golden Wisdom Temple. Then I looked out the doors and I saw Z (the spiritual name for the Mahanta is Wah Z, often shortened to just Z) coming and I said, "Hey, Z!" and he said, "Come here." He took me over to a wall, and there were two mirrors there. They were lined up, one above the other.

He told me to look into the mirrors. I looked in both mirrors and could see my image in the top and bottom mirrors at the same time. I saw two different reflections. The top reflection was *not* how I would normally look. My hair was different and I was wearing different clothes than I usually do. The bottom reflection was how I usually looked and dressed. Z said, "Which one is you?"

It was a realization to me that I was not acting like who I was. I was trying to be someone different. That ended the experience, because I knew what he was getting at. It was like I knew that I wasn't being myself. I had been shown an image so I could understand.

THE REALITY OF A CHILD'S IMAGINATION

Parents who do not know about the reality of Soul Travel, past lives, and dreams may discourage children

Parents who do not know about the reality of Soul Travel, past lives, and dreams may discourage children from speaking of their experiences because they seem far-fetched.

from speaking of their experiences because they seem
far-fetched. They may say, "Oh, that's just your imagination." But Harold Klemp says:

> *Children at an early age often remember
> past lives, and they'll tell you about them, if
> you're their parent. Just ask them a question
> like, What were you last time when you were big?
> They'll come up with some very interesting an-
> swers. If you just listen and make believe you are
> the child listening to a great sage, you can learn
> a lot from children.*[3]

Luckily, some of us remember our youthful jour-
neys into the heavenly worlds of God. Sabrina has
some very early memories of Soul Travel:

My first clear memory in this lifetime was
when I was a baby, just a few months old.
This memory was just a clear awareness, like a
remembrance: "I am not my body. I know I'm in
a baby's body, but this is not who I am." I could
hear and even understand everything being said
around me, and knew I was a spiritual being,
more than a baby.

When I was six months old, I was taken to
the doctor's and put on a scale to be weighed.
The doctor and my mother tried to get me to lie
down, but I didn't want to. For some reason, I
just wanted to sit up. I was curious about where
I was. They kept trying to get me to lie down,
but by the third try, I sat up again and just
popped out of my body. I was looking at my
mother and the doctor from out of my body. As
a baby, I thought this was normal. It seemed

*If you just
listen and make
believe you are
the child
listening to a
great sage, you
can learn a lot
from children.*

totally natural to me. I remembered this all my life. Soul Travel *is* natural!

My father, who was only with me the first six years of my life, helped me remember the inner worlds. He told me if I closed my eyes, I would see a beam of light. He also said I could meet him in the dream state. He helped me keep the link to Holy Spirit open.

When I was eighteen, I found out about Soul Travel through Eckankar.

I'm so grateful to my dad for helping me to become a seeker of truth and a finder of real freedom—spiritual freedom.

Here's an exercise parents can use to validate children's Soul Travel experiences and learn from the child as well:

Here's an exercise parents can use to validate children's Soul Travel experiences.

Soul Travel Exercise:

Fostering the Wisdom of Youth

1. Ask your child if he has experienced flying, or other beautiful things, in dreams.

2. Ask if he would like to know how to have more of these pleasant experiences and avoid the bad ones (like nightmares). If he says yes, teach him to sing HU, as explained on page 13.

3. Explain that singing HU is a way to lift yourself into the most beautiful places, closer to where your true home is as Soul. In the physical world, here on earth, we are limited in our physical bodies, but when we Soul Travel in

> dreams or other ways, we are on spiritual adventures. Sing HU along with your child to show him how.

VALIDATION FOR CHILDHOOD SOUL TRAVEL

I remember being out of my body when I was in first and second grade. This was mostly because I was called back into my body regularly by my teacher. Then when I grew up, I got validation that I had gone somewhere:

In first and second grade I was called back into my body regularly by my teacher.

When I was in first and second grade I was reprimanded by my teacher for daydreaming. Since I wasn't very happy with my new foster family, and I was in a strange new school, I escaped by Soul Traveling, though I didn't know that's what it was at the time.

I imagined playing in the hills. I was with a friend, but I didn't know who. When I grew up, I met someone who instantly became a dear friend. She told me of her childhood playmate. Her invisible playmate was small and dark haired (like me) and named Debbie! Her parents would even set a place at the table for Debbie, as my friend insisted they do. She is absolutely sure it was me.

My friend and I have known each other many lifetimes and established a love bond. Her love helped me adjust to my new life by giving me little Soul Travel vacations away in the hills with an old and trusted friend.

Out-of-body experiences can be subtle. A person

might not even know it has occurred until later, looking back on the event, like I did.

INTEREST IN SOUL TRAVEL CAN BEGIN ANYTIME

My interest in spiritual matters started when I was small, about six years old. I knew there was beauty, mystery, and life beyond this life. I knew this every time I saw a Disney movie or read a fairy tale. I knew by the tingling feeling I got that there was something much more wonderful than schoolbooks or Barbie dolls. Somehow, I had to find it!

At age twelve I heard there were books on reincarnation and read every one I could find.

When I was in college, I read every book I could get my hands on that spoke of other worlds and senses beyond the normal. I knew that there was more to life than what we could see, hear, or touch.

Then I began a custom of going into my room in the evening before dinner for some quiet time alone. I would close my dark blue curtains and watch the light filter through them, creating a soft blue glow. I would then close my eyes and simply look within. I had no idea what I was doing. I had never been taught to meditate, contemplate, or do spiritual exercises, though I had heard of meditation and taken one-day classes in various spiritual teachings. But I knew that what I was doing was different.

One day I felt there was a being of light sitting across from me on my bed, his legs crossed under him, just as mine were. I felt so good and uplifted I couldn't bear it. I had to open my eyes. I had felt a

Out-of-body experiences can be subtle. A person might not even know it has occurred until later, looking back on the event.

presence, yet no one was there!

The next time I did this exercise, I remember thinking of a good friend I dearly loved. At that very moment, the phone rang. One of my roommates knocked on the door and said, "It's for you." It was the friend I'd been thinking of!

I knew in my heart this was confirmation of my evening exercise. There was something going on beyond my physical senses and awareness, but what?

A few months later I found Eckankar, which explained everything to me. I was ecstatic! Now I had real tools to go beyond this world, into that wonderfully real inner world I had only hoped for in my childhood. I was free!

YOUTHFUL SOUL TRAVEL DREAMS

Dreams, like John's below, can also turn to Soul Travel experiences, especially when you use spiritual tools like the word *HU*:

> I dreamed I could hardly move. Then I saw my mom and brother. They said calmly, "Sing HU in a bad dream, and you can have God's protection."

When I was little my parents talked about HU (ancient name for God described on page 13.) They also said it could actually be good to have bad dreams. Just a few years ago, when I was about thirteen, I dreamed that I was in a store, walking along and looking through the shelves. Suddenly an armed robber came in and began chasing me.

I could hardly move, no matter how hard I tried to run! Then I saw my mom and my brother. They said calmly, "Sing HU in a bad dream, and you can have God's protection." So I sang HU.

Out of the corner of my eye, I saw my father,

mother, and sister sitting at a table smiling at me. I knew then everything was OK. Then I turned around to see where the thief was, and he was gone! My family's love took the place of any fear I had, and my family was all that remained in the dream.

Soul Travel in this dream was a simple shift in consciousness from fear to love by using the song of HU—the easiest method of all. Dreams can be a great way to prove to yourself that shifting to God's love can create a quick shift in your life. In dreams it can be instantaneous, so it can illustrate the theory in a dramatic way.

Soul Travel in this dream was a simple shift in consciousness from fear to love by using the song of HU—the easiest method of all.

Soul Travel Exercise:

Change the Dream with HU

For parents to help young children, or for older children to help themselves with scary or uncomfortable dreams, sing HU! It's just that simple. (See explanation of HU on page 13.) Sing HU in a long, drawn-out breath, on any musical note you wish. It is pronounced like the word *hue*. HU-U-U-U.

Fifteen-year-old Sonya helps herself go to sleep by imagining the sound of violins. She loves music, so it helps her to feel uplifted and have wonderful dreams. Would you like to try an exercise that may help you shift into Soul consciousness more easily before sleep? If so, try this next exercise tonight:

Soul Travel Exercise: Dance to the Music

1. Think of some musical instrument or sound you love to hear. Perhaps it's someone singing.

2. Simply put your attention on the beauty of the music as you drift off to sleep. Think of how it uplifts you. Even dance to it inwardly, feeling the movement as Soul.

From the time I was a young Soul Traveler in my twenties, I loved dancing inwardly with my spiritual guide, the Mahanta, or by myself. I found myself flying and leaping in ways I could never do in the physical world. Also, I could visit places I never knew existed.

Some young Soul Travelers (ages ten to thirteen), members of a family I knew, introduced me to a very special place to visit in the inner heavenly worlds. They called it Crystal Moon Palace. Indeed, I found that other children knew of this place.

It was a Temple of Golden Wisdom made of crystal. There were beautiful gardens with flowers whose beauty surpassed any you would find on earth. The light of an other-worldly moon glowed through the crystal, creating a special effect. As Soul, children played in their own wonderland while their physical bodies slept.

Have you ever felt unworthy of God's love, or fearful about your life? Having a spiritual guide helped me let go of my fears.

ACCEPTING GOD'S LOVE AND PROTECTION

Have you ever felt unworthy of God's love, or fearful about your life? Having a spiritual guide helped me let go of my fears. You can do it too, simply by asking for guidance and love in your life. Try this next exercise to let go of fear and make room for love:

Spiritual Exercise: Letting Go of Fear

1. Imagine the greatest spiritual guide, teacher, and protector. What would he look like? If you want to, you can ask the Mahanta to be your guide. Imagine the great love that flows from him as he looks at you with eternal, unconditional love.

2. Look at the fear you may feel inside. Take it out, and put it inside a box. Wrap the box, and hand it to your spiritual guide as a gift. The gift is that you have given up the fear to make more room for God's love. The Mahanta, or your spiritual guide, takes the gift and tosses it into the holy fire of God's love.

   Imagine this any way you want. You could imagine the gift turning into sparkles of divine love, changing the fear into love. Do this as often as you need to.

If you want to, you can ask the Mahanta to be your guide.

God's love saved Allen when he was seventeen. He had to trust and accept this love instantly as he took a quick trip on the Time Track, a few seconds into the future:

As a child I learned to Soul Travel consciously, or perhaps I just remembered what was natural to Soul. While my body was in the classroom, my real self, Soul, was playing in the hills near my home. This practice may have saved my life later, when I was a teen.

A friend and I once rode our motorcycles from Santa Cruz to San Jose. We were going way too fast. A trip that should have taken us forty minutes only took eighteen! As we rounded a sharp curve, I was instantly out of my body, viewing the oncoming traffic. I would not have been able to see any of this with my physical eyes. Everything was in slow motion then, as if time had been suspended.

I could see a truck moving too fast. Then I actually saw the future in a split second. The truck would fishtail into my lane due to his speed. I immediately swung wide into the outside curve, avoiding sure death.

Had I not seen the whole incident from the Soul perspective, above time and space, I would never have swung that wide. I'm so grateful for the viewpoint of Soul.

Time and space are an illusion. We can rise above them as Soul to see what's ahead.

As Allen discovered, time and space are an illusion. We can rise above them as Soul to see what's ahead. Maya was protected in a similar way:

As a child I remember being very independent, almost a rebel. If someone said the sky was blue, I would say it was green. If I didn't have the experience someone else did, I didn't feel like I should believe it unless I had my own experience. I learned to always check inside to see what was real and true for me, deep down.

When I was in third grade, we had to walk about a quarter mile to our school bus stop and cross a very busy road. One day I had a feeling. I just knew I could not cross that road. This feeling came out of nowhere. It came so fast, it was just a part of me. I could not move. The other kids went across in that moment, and a semi-trailer truck going very fast came out of nowhere, just as fast as that feeling in me had come. The other kids barely made it across the road. I knew then why I had that feeling.

Now I know what the feeling was. I was being lifted out of my body to see what was going to happen, so I could avoid being hurt. I was so used to tuning in as Soul, that I was seeing and hearing from that greater viewpoint.

I was being lifted out of my body to see what was going to happen, so I could avoid being hurt.

EXPLORING THE UNIVERSE

Michael searched his mind and went beyond it to explore the universe as much as he could:

When I was twelve years old, I was so curious about reality I would get headaches thinking about it! There were men going into space and walking on the moon. I wondered about the universe—things like, what's beyond the edge? If the universe is only so big, it has to have an edge. I was just thinking about it mentally. What I learned about the universe was not quite jelling for me. I wondered why it wasn't.

I would ask myself, If the physical universe is everything, where does it end? How far does it go? If it's infinite, how infinite is it?

I just knew there was more than the physical universe. I could see there was more there, but as soon as I got close to it, my mind would pull me back. I wasn't ready to experience that greater consciousness. I was seeing, as Soul, a higher plane, a greater reality, but I didn't know it!

The next chapter shows you how you can explore the universe of God and the heavenly worlds that are right in front of you, right in your own home, your own neighborhood!

7

Beyond Soul Travel— Living in Heaven Now

Heaven is not a place as much as it is your state of consciousness.

— Harold Klemp, *The Dream Master*,
Mahanta Transcripts, Book 8[1]

$\mathscr{A}$s you have likely surmised by now, Soul Traveling to find God's love can be as simple as shifting your viewpoint from the mundane to the miraculous in any moment.

One winter day, for example, as I gazed out the window, I remembered to think of God's love in nature. Then it happened! Suddenly, a bird in flight was a spiritual being. Its little wings were spread in joy. Its song echoed divine love, and I could almost feel its heart beat with the Life Force that flowed through it from the heavenly worlds. I was feeling the love of God in that precious, simple expression of freedom.

We don't have to go anywhere but here to experience God's love.

God's Love Here and Now

We don't have to go anywhere but here to experience God's love. Just thinking of Soul Travel can

115

shift us to a higher viewpoint or awareness. It helps us see more of the divine in every situation, and we can Soul Travel while wide awake and very conscious. Soul Travel, at higher levels of awareness, is not so much about travel. It's about shifting awareness, knowing, and being in a high state of unconditional, divine love.

Here's an example of how another bird brought someone else deeper into this precious love from God. Chelsea experienced this divine love in a single moment:

Soul Travel, at higher levels of awareness, is not so much about travel. It's about shifting awareness, knowing, and being in a high state of divine love.

After two days of an autumn snow the trees were piled high with it. Every branch was covered in at least two inches of heavy, wet snow. The birds had nowhere to perch.

Then I saw a miracle! A bird landed on a branch that somehow had about three clean inches, the only snow-free piece of branch anywhere around. That branch was right outside my window. For some reason, that sweet bird for whom God had provided a small resting place touched my heart and made me soar. It seemed God was sending me love through this tiny creature. I felt so much awe in this experience. As Soul, I was definitely connecting with God's love in that moment.

Later, I got validation of my experience when I was speaking on the phone to someone at the Internal Revenue Service to straighten something out. I thanked her for being so kind. The last two people I had spoken with treated me rudely, speaking sternly and angrily. That had confused and disturbed me. Were they having a bad day, or was this the way they were trained? But this third IRS agent was very pleasant.

Suddenly, a beautiful cardinal flew onto the snow-free piece of branch right outside my window, and I felt so much love I had to share it. I mentioned it to the agent. She said, "Oh, I love when other people notice those things! Those small things are so important."

I ventured to say, "I believe it's God's love speaking to us."

"Oh yes!" she agreed. Then she proceeded to give me a wonderful solution to solving my income-tax riddle—something no other agent had been able to do in five years!

The love I experienced from God through those two birds lifted me up out of my limiting thoughts and attitudes and gave me a fresh feeling of being clean and new in that very moment, sparkling as Soul.

Would you like to try an exercise to experience God's love right here and now in this physical level of heaven?

Would you like to try an exercise to experience God's love right here and now?

Soul Travel Exercise:

Everyday Soul Travel— Connecting with God's Love

1. What kinds of everyday occurrences make you happy? List them now. It can be as common as getting a pen that writes smoothly, or a smile from a child or stranger. Perhaps it's someone holding the elevator for you, or a restaurant

server who goes one step more to help you. Maybe it's nature's wonders or a satisfying meal, driving a smooth road or seeing a good movie. Whatever small things you love, take note.

Also, remember when you have given love to another, no matter how small the act of kindness, and notice how it opened your heart to God's love and blessings.

2. Look at these things as God's way of sending you love. Notice how you feel uplifted, even a little, out of your everyday way of feeling and thinking. Look at the gift of God's love while remembering that moment, and look for God's love the next time it occurs.

This small shift in consciousness, no matter how minor it might seem at the time, can be a real Soul Travel experience. It is Soul experiencing God's love in that moment. It can be a reminder that this is also one of the levels of heaven and you, Soul, are residing and traveling here as well!

How can we keep this higher view of life, the heavenly view from the perspective of Soul?

KEEPING THE FOCUS

How can we keep this higher view of life, the heavenly view from the perspective of Soul?

One easy way is to stay connected to God and the Holy Spirit through daily spiritual exercises, like those taught in Eckankar. There are several in this book, quoted from the writings of Harold Klemp. You can find lots more in his book *The Spiritual Exercises of ECK.*

Leah, like many people who study Eckankar, finds that her spiritual exercises are a great advantage in her life:

I wouldn't be here in the United States, doing what I love, if I didn't do my spiritual exercises daily. Doing spiritual exercises consistently keeps the inner connection open to divine guidance whenever I need it.

Because I listen to the direction of the Holy Spirit, I went from not knowing anyone in this country, being broke and not knowing where to go, to having a job and a place to stay. What's even more amazing is that the person I stayed with was an old friend who spoke my native language. And the job I got was my dream job, teaching ballet for a ballet company!

I used to fall asleep when I did my spiritual exercises; now I don't. I may not always sit for the full twenty minutes, as recommended, but I'm consistent about doing the exercises every day. Also, during the day I try to find a quiet moment to connect with Spirit. I might be dancing, looking at the Mahanta's picture, or reading uplifting spiritual material, like Eckankar books.

Before I found Eckankar and the spiritual exercises, I was longing for truth and freedom. Now that I have found them and this wonderful connection with Divine Spirit, I could never do without it or neglect it. When I keep the connection open, I can hear the Holy Spirit better. I still make mistakes once in a while, but generally I am doing much better.

Doing spiritual exercises consistently keeps the inner connection open to divine guidance whenever I need it.

It's good to find anything that can get us out of our daily rush and hurry and busyness. Just to find a moment to stop and remember that there are higher things behind our daily lives. I hope I never forget that.

As long as someone wants to remember and practices some sort of daily discipline like the spiritual exercises, as Leah does, life reminds us of what is important. Here's a tip from the expert, Harold Klemp. It is from his book *The Art of Spiritual Dreaming*[2].

Spiritual exercises are like physical exercises: Before your muscles grow strong, you have to exercise them a number of times. From the moment you begin, changes are being made in you.

Tip: It Takes Practice

If the spiritual exercises don't work the first time, do them again and again. They are like physical exercises: Before your muscles grow strong, you have to exercise them a number of times; it doesn't always happen in one try. It's quite likely that if you take up an exercise routine for thirty days, you're going to be stronger than you were in the beginning.

It's the same way with the spiritual exercises. The purpose of the Spiritual Exercises of ECK is simply to open a conduit or a channel between yourself and the Holy Spirit. From the moment you begin chanting and looking for truth in this particular way, whether you are conscious of it or not, changes are being made in you.

Serving God to Live in Heaven

Monks or yogis may retreat for years or go into seclusion, but doing the Spiritual Exercises of ECK inspires one to serve God in daily life. I once went through a period where I felt, more and more, the need to serve God. I also wanted to grow spiritually in order to be a greater vehicle for God's love. That is a constant, ongoing process, and I know I will keep learning forever. But one experience I had, described below, helped me see the great need for patience in the process, especially patience with myself. I also learned to be more careful about what I ask for.

Doing the Spiritual Exercises of ECK inspires one to serve God in daily life.

Soon after I started studying Eckankar, I wondered about a certain saying I noticed: The spiritual student does more and more about less and less, and the spiritual master does less and less about more and more. It was about this time that my health took a downturn. At the same time, I became very interested in the spiritual Law of Economy. The Law of Economy means we make good use of our energy while staying in harmony with life. I thought I was pretty good at this, at the time.

I kept asking the Mahanta, my inner spiritual master, what I could do to improve my health. It seemed I went to every kind of health practitioner in the world, from chiropractors to acupuncturists, to naturopaths, to general practitioners. Nothing seemed to help me. But one practitioner (who was also my former husband) did comment on the way I worked. He said my health would only improve when I learned to work differently.

I knew what he meant. I was frantic in the way I worked. I was like a windup toy that ran and ran and ran and never stopped until I ran out of energy completely. Then I would collapse. I'd do three things at once, all very quickly, even when I didn't feel I could take another step. I thought this was how I had to work in order to survive.

My health kept getting worse. I'd collapse and have to take a nap twice a day many days. Then I couldn't seem to sleep at night, no matter how exhausted I was. I was very distraught over not having energy. I only felt like a fully capable human being about one day per year. Yet I tried to stay positive. After all, I had written self-help books all about that! I had to walk my talk, didn't I? Besides, I needed to make a living.

Still, I got weaker and less able to work or even do as much volunteer work. I begged the Inner Master for help. I pleaded with him to show me what I was doing that kept my health from improving. After all, I was serving God, wasn't I?

I forgot that serving God also meant serving myself with love—treating myself as a spiritual being with all the rights to a balanced life that any other spiritual being has. This means all of us.

Since I had to work less and do more, I began to learn many shortcuts. Through Soul Travel, I learned the Law of Economy (you can learn more about this spiritual law and many others in Harold Klemp's book *The Spiritual Laws of Life*,[3] which is an important tool for spiritual unfoldment). As I lay in bed in the morning, floating through the

> Serving God also meant serving myself with love—treating myself as a spiritual being with all the rights to a balanced life that any other spiritual being has.

day ahead in the Soul body, I would imagine how I could do a certain task, and suddenly I would see the shortcut.

I would see how it could be done much more easily and quickly, using less energy, time, and even fewer materials. I could see from this perspective when it was wise to sit back and let things come to me. Let others call me back, for instance, instead of chasing people down (as was typical of my type A personality).

I started to relax more about life and found that I was actually earning more money working fewer hours!

Through the Mahanta's great love and guidance, I was able to accept new ways of working and living in a more calm, relaxed manner. My question, how to do less and less about more and more, was answered through experience. I had no choice but to slow down, and I saw how much more effective it was to work that way. I am eternally thankful for all the love and inner peace I received from God in this experience.

THE LIGHT OF GOD ON EARTH

Many people have experienced God's love as a simple, precious Blue Light. Harold Klemp explains:

> *Those of you in Eckankar are very familiar with the Blue Light. This is a sign of the Holy Spirit, the Sound and Light of God speaking to the individual. Sometimes It comes as Light and sometimes It comes as Sound. Sometimes It comes as both.*

Many people have experienced God's love as a simple, precious Blue Light.

The Inner Master is the matrix that the Holy Spirit forms. The Mahanta is the Inner Master, the inner side. The Living ECK Master is the outer side. People often see the Inner Master first come to them as the Blue Light. This is very common, because they're not yet ready to see the face of the Inner Master, the Mahanta. It would shock them too much.

In some way the Holy Spirit, the ECK, speaks to the individual through Light or Sound. The Light may be any color, but when It shows up as the Blue Light, It's very definitely the Mahanta.

Sometimes the Light is yellow, which is a high spiritual color, and white, even higher. Or it may be a pink or orange light, and sometimes a violet or purple light. Orange is the Causal Plane—the past-life memory area. But to see the Blue Light is a special blessing.

Whenever a person sees any of these lights inwardly, either during contemplation, in meditation, or in a dream, this is very important. The Holy Spirit is uplifting them spiritually. The Light doesn't just come. It's not just a colored filter put in front of some sort of lightbulb. It's there for a reason.

It's to uplift that Soul into a higher state of consciousness.[4]

> The Light may be any color, but when It shows up as the Blue Light, It's very definitely the Mahanta. To see the Blue Light is a special blessing.

Mark saw a blue light that changed his life:

*M*any years before I knew about the Light and Sound of God, I was living in a trailer, depressed and down on my luck. I had no job and no money coming in. I knew that there was nowhere to turn but God. Yet I wondered if God even existed, or cared, for that matter. It was a dark night, nothing to lift my mood. I looked outside the window, thinking, *What could be out there for me? Is there anything at all?*

The next thing I knew there was a blue light across the street, like a soft, warm bulb, glowing in that blackness. I had never noticed a blue lightbulb on anyone's trailer. Where had it come from?

For some reason, I knew it was there to make me feel better. I felt so much love. I thought I was imagining things when the bulb became larger and brighter. Though it was cold, I walked outside in my thin shirt, to get a better look and to assure myself that it was indeed just a lightbulb.

When I reached the place I thought the bulb should be, it was further on ahead. *What's going on?* I thought. *Am I going crazy? That would certainly fit right in with my string of bad luck.* But I felt so much love from that blue light!

I went home thinking about it. Later I fell asleep and dreamed about the blue light. When I woke up in the morning, I felt like I lived in a whole different world! My mood lightened and I felt hopeful again. I began to look for work and found it! Heaven had come to earth to help me, and I was truly blessed.

Gina's life changed, too, when she found the Light of God right here on earth:

When I was going through a tough time, I saw the Light of God. I was a nurse working the night shift. I had just sustained four major losses in my life: my marriage, custody of my two children, and my twin sister's death. I couldn't

> I felt so much love from that blue light! When I woke up in the morning, I felt like I lived in a whole different world!

have gotten much further down than I was. I didn't believe in anything in particular, especially right then!

A nurse I had never met came onto the floor to work that night. I don't normally see spiritual things, but I saw a light around her that was so bright I had to ask her about it. I said, "What is that light around you?"

She told me it was the ECK, or Holy Spirit—that it was the Light and Sound of God. My life changed completely in that moment. I found what I had always been looking for. I found heaven on earth when I met that woman with the beautiful light who showed me how to get back to who I really was, Soul.

I've learned since then that we have to clear out the old things before we can see better things ahead. We need to let go of the heavy load and move on. The illusion about what you are supposed to have in your life and when is shattered. Then the gifts come and keep on coming—more than you could ever imagine!

You can experience the Light of God anytime, anyplace. Try the next exercise for one solid week if you'd like to see results.

> You can experience the Light of God anytime, anyplace.

Soul Travel Exercise: Looking for the Light

1. While doing some daily task outside, like driving, shoveling snow, raking leaves, or going for a walk, ask yourself, "Where do I see light?"

2. Trust yourself to see the Light of God in everyday occurrences. You may find this divine Light

suddenly pops up when you least expect it, where you least expect it, just because you have been looking in earnest.

Helen saw the Light of God in nature, knowing it was divine. She faced a challenge to her survival and was able to replace fear with love and find joy in the midst of adversity:

I had just been told that my twelve-year job was coming to an end. I felt terrible. My job was the only thing in my life that hadn't changed after divorce, weight issues, and other things. Now my manager was telling me I wasn't performing at the level they wanted. I had six months to "shape up or ship out."

Six months was not nearly enough time to see results in retail buying. For example, products from a buying trip in January would be delivered in September. Sales figures would not show until much later than six months. What was I to do?

Even though I had been in this business for twenty-six years, I knew that retail buying wasn't the greatest career for me. I wasn't that good at it. I had to leave work right away that afternoon to drive somewhere. I happened to drive through a woods on my way. It was a gorgeous spring day, and the sun was shining brightly through the new leaves on the trees.

As soon as I saw that, I knew this was a huge opportunity for me. In that moment, I felt the love of God. Heaven was with me. I knew the Mahanta, my spiritual guide, would provide for me—and he did!

You may find this divine Light suddenly pops up when you least expect it, just because you have been looking in earnest.

Not only did I get a vacation with three months' severance pay, I also had time to think about what I really wanted. What could be more heavenly?

Paying Attention to Heaven

Heaven is here on earth for those who can see it.

The gifts of Spirit may be subtle—not gold or diamonds, but simple, childlike treasures. As a child, Mimi found them in her heart:

> *W*hen I was a kid I loved trees. I loved going off by myself and climbing the biggest tree, going to the very top. I would climb out onto the longest limb, all the way to the very end. It scared everyone in my family. But that's where I felt closest to God.
>
> What I was told about God in church, that He was someone to be afraid of, was dissolved when I went up to the top of that tree. I felt safe and loved. The limbs felt like the arms of God giving me protection and love.
>
> That changed my feeling about God from then on. God wasn't something to be feared, but loved.

When our hearts are open, soft, and childlike enough to let God in, we can have all the love we want, here and now, on this very level of heaven.

To experience more of God's love now, try this spiritual exercise for direct knowingness. It is from Harold Klemp's book *The Art of Spiritual Dreaming*[5].

The gifts of Spirit may be subtle—not gold or diamonds, but simple, childlike treasures.

Soul Travel Exercise:

For Direct Knowingness

Those who have Soul Traveled may now want to go to the higher state of direct knowingness, without having to go through the intermediary stages. Dreams and Soul Travel are helpful and important, but at some point you outgrow them.

Simply chant the words *divine love*, letter by letter. Originally I was going to give it as L-O-V-E, but some people would mix it up with human love. The word *divine* takes it beyond human love. Divine love brings you all forms of love, including human love. To limit it to the usual definition of love is like working from the bottom, instead of working from the top of spirituality.

So, chant D-I-V-I-N-E L-O-V-E. This means you seek the highest form of love, which brings all blessings to you.

Simply chant the words *divine love*, letter by letter: D-I-V-I-N-E L-O-V-E. This means you seek the highest form of love, which brings all blessings to you.

Jen did a spiritual exercise like the one above. Her heart opened to divine love, leaving her with a greater understanding of how she had prevented herself from experiencing more:

was so excited when I finally realized how I had been limiting myself in my awareness and acceptance of divine love. Now I could open more fully to it. A friend had mentioned to me that I might try to imagine that my heart was a flower and envision it opening like the petals of a flower. I had tried this before without much success. Now I thought to myself, *Why don't I open my whole self?*

I imagined opening up my whole body to the ECK, Holy Spirit. Then I imagined opening myself, as Soul, to the whole universe, then to all universes and heavenly planes. I felt so free! I felt this neutral kind of love. It felt so good as I surrendered to it and opened heart, mind, and body more and more. I felt my life changing from that simple act of opening to this incredible love. After trying for years to find the secret, it was so simple!

I suddenly realized that all of my health problems were from the heart down. I had been limiting the flow of the Holy Spirit! I knew immediately that opening up to this flow would help my health and many other areas of my life. This would happen as I could accept more and more of God's pure, divine love. I got a better understanding of these words from the Bible: "But rather seek ye the kingdom of God; and all these things shall be added unto you."[6]

I felt I had found the key to another biblical statement: "the kingdom of God is within you."[7]

I also saw something very important to me. How to live in heaven *now*. How to live on many levels of heaven at once. As I expanded upward and outward, I felt the reality of many levels of awareness all at once, and the presence of God in them all. It felt so good to know that I was unlimited as a spiritual being, as Soul—that I could grow and unfold eternally.

Giving and receiving become one ecstatic circle in the flow of ECK, or Holy Spirit. When we are open

When we are open to giving and receiving unconditional divine love, we can experience heaven now.

to giving and receiving unconditional divine love, we can experience heaven now. It may take diligence, attention, and the desire to see the divine in the seemingly mundane. It might take a willingness to find heaven in any moment, in any circumstance or situation. And it may require a more open heart like that of a child, believing that you are loved, always, by God, and giving that love back to others.

It's completely possible to do all of these things. Many others have, so why not you?

Harold Klemp says:

> *Whoever seeks God with a pure heart shall find Him. This promise of the ancient ECK Masters is renewed today.*
>
> *We learn first by dreams. Then, by one of the many aspects of Soul Travel, whether it includes the fantastic out-of-the-body experience or something more subtle. After that comes our first important spiritual realization, which is from the Soul Plane.*
>
> *And finally, if Soul desires God badly enough, It enters God Consciousness.*[8]

If your goal is to find God's love, you will.

If your goal is to find God's love, you will. Much love to you on your journey!

Glossary

Words set in SMALL CAPS are defined elsewhere in this glossary.

BLUE LIGHT.   How the MAHANTA often appears in the inner worlds to the CHELA or seeker.

CHELA. *CHEE-lah*   A spiritual student. Often refers to a member of ECKANKAR.

ECK. *EHK*   The Life Force, the Holy Spirit, or Audible Life Current which sustains all life.

ECKANKAR. *EHK-ahn-kahr*   Religion of the Light and Sound of God. Also known as the Ancient Science of SOUL TRAVEL. A truly spiritual religion for the individual in modern times. The teachings provide a framework for anyone to explore their own spiritual experiences. Established by PAUL TWITCHELL, the modern-day founder, in 1965. The word means "Co-worker with God."

ECK MASTER(S).   Spiritual Masters who can assist and protect people in their spiritual studies and travels. The ECK Masters are from a long line of God-Realized SOULS who know the responsibility that goes with spiritual freedom.

GOD-REALIZATION.   The state of God Consciousness. Complete and conscious awareness of God.

HU. *HYOO*   The most ancient, secret name for God. The singing of the word *HU* is considered a love song to God. It can be sung aloud or silently to oneself.

INITIATION.   Earned by a member of ECKANKAR through spiritual unfoldment and service to God. The initiation is a private ceremony in which the individual is linked to the Sound and Light of God.

KAL NIRANJAN, THE. *KAL nee-RAHN-jahn*   The Kal; the negative power, also known as Satan or the devil.

KARMA, LAW OF.   The Law of Cause and Effect, action and reaction, justice, retribution, and reward, which applies to the lower or psychic worlds: the Physical, Astral, Causal, Mental, and Etheric Planes.

KLEMP, HAROLD. The present MAHANTA, the LIVING ECK MASTER. SRI Harold Klemp became the Mahanta, the Living ECK Master in 1981. His spiritual name is WAH Z.

LAI TSI. *lie TSEE* An ancient Chinese ECK Master.

LIVING ECK MASTER. The title of the spiritual leader of ECKANKAR. His duty is to lead SOUL back to God. The Living ECK Master can assist spiritual students physically as the Outer Master, in the dream state as the Dream Master, and in the spiritual worlds as the Inner Master.

MAHANTA. *mah-HAHN-tah* A title to describe the highest state of God Consciousness on earth, often embodied in the LIVING ECK MASTER. He is the Living Word. An expression of the Spirit of God that is always with you. Sometimes seen as a Blue Light or Blue Star or in the form of the Mahanta, the Living ECK Master.

PLANE(S). The levels of existence, such as the Physical, Astral, Causal, Mental, Etheric, and SOUL Planes.

REBAZAR TARZS. *REE-bah-zahr TAHRZ* A Tibetan ECK MASTER known as the torchbearer of ECKANKAR in the lower worlds.

SELF-REALIZATION. SOUL recognition. The entering of Soul into the Soul PLANE and there beholding Itself as pure Spirit. A state of seeing, knowing, and being.

SHARIYAT-KI-SUGMAD. *SHAH-ree-aht-kee-SOOG-mahd* The sacred scriptures of ECKANKAR. The scriptures are comprised of about twelve volumes in the spiritual worlds. The first two were transcribed from the inner PLANES by PAUL TWITCHELL, modern-day founder of ECKANKAR.

SOUL. The True Self. The inner, most sacred part of each person. Soul exists before birth and lives on after the death of the physical body. As a spark of God, Soul can see, know, and perceive all things. It is the creative center of Its own world.

SOUL TRAVEL. The expansion of consciousness. The ability of SOUL to transcend the physical body and travel into the spiritual worlds of God. Soul Travel is taught only by the LIVING ECK MASTER. It helps people unfold spiritually and can provide proof of the existence of God and life after death.

SOUND AND LIGHT OF ECK. The Holy Spirit. The two aspects through which God appears in the lower worlds. People can experience them by looking and listening within themselves and through SOUL TRAVEL.

SPIRITUAL EXERCISES OF ECK. The daily practice of certain techniques to get us in touch with the Light and Sound of God.

SRI. *SREE* A title of spiritual respect, similar to reverend or pastor, used for those who have attained the Kingdom of God. In ECKANKAR, it is reserved for the MAHANTA, the LIVING ECK MASTER.

SUGMAD. *SOOG-mahd*   A sacred name for God. Sugmad is neither masculine nor feminine; It is the source of all life.

TEMPLE(S) OF GOLDEN WISDOM. These Golden Wisdom Temples are spiritual temples which exist on the various PLANES—from the Physical to the Anami Lok; CHELAS of ECKANKAR are taken to the temples in the SOUL body to be educated in the divine knowledge; the different sections of the SHARIYAT-KI-SUGMAD, the sacred teachings of ECK, are kept at these temples.

TWITCHELL, PAUL. An American ECK MASTER who brought the modern teachings of ECKANKAR to the world through his writings and lectures. His spiritual name is Peddar Zaskq.

For more explanations of ECKANKAR terms, see *A Cosmic Sea of Words: The ECKANKAR Lexicon* by Harold Klemp.

Notes

Introduction.

1. Anita Bartholomew, "After Life," *Reader's Digest*, August 2003, 122–28.
2. Harold Klemp, "The Power of Love," Minneapolis: ECKANKAR Worldwide Seminar, October 13, 2001. Audio recording.
3. B. G. DeSylva, Lew Brown & Ray Henderson, "The Best Things In Life Are Free," 1927.
4. Paul Twitchell, *ECKANKAR—The Key to Secret Worlds*, 2d ed. (Minneapolis: ECKANKAR, 1969, 1987).
5. Harold Klemp, *Past Lives, Dreams, and Soul Travel* (Minneapolis: ECKANKAR, 2003).
6. Harold Klemp, *How to Survive Spiritually in Our Times*, Mahanta Transcripts, Book 16 (Minneapolis: ECKANKAR, 2001), 202.

Chapter 1. Soul Travel to Find Heaven Now

1. Harold Klemp, *What Is Spiritual Freedom?* Mahanta Transcripts, Book 11 (Minneapolis: ECKANKAR, 1995), 11–12.
2. 2 Corinthians 12:2 Authorized (King James) Version.
3. Harold Klemp, *Our Spiritual Wake-Up Calls*, Mahanta Transcripts, Book 15 (Minneapolis: ECKANKAR, 1997), 176–77.
4. Klemp, *How to Survive Spiritually in Our Times*, 248.
5. Harold Klemp, *How the Inner Master Works*, Mahanta Transcripts, Book 12 (Minneapolis: ECKANKAR, 1995), 75.
6. Harold Klemp, *Those Wonderful ECK Masters* (Minneapolis: ECKANKAR, 2005).

Chapter 2. A Variety of Ways to Soul Travel

1. Klemp, *What Is Spiritual Freedom?* 5.
2. Harold Klemp, *The Art of Spiritual Dreaming* (Minneapolis: ECKANKAR, 1999), 271.
3. Harold Klemp, *ECK Wisdom Temples, Spiritual Cities, & Guides: A Brief History* (Minneapolis: ECKANKAR, 2000).
4. Debbie Johnson, *Exploring Past Lives to Heal the Present* (Minneapolis: ECKANKAR, 2004).

5. Harold Klemp, *The Living Word*, Book 1 (Minneapolis: ECKANKAR, 1989), 148–49.

Chapter 3. Practical Soul Travel

1. Harold Klemp, *The Golden Heart*, Mahanta Transcripts, Book 4 (Minneapolis: ECKANKAR, 1990), 57.
2. Mary Carroll Moore, *How to Master Change in Your Life: Sixty-seven Ways to Handle Life's Toughest Moments* (Minneapolis: ECKANKAR, 1997), 76–77.
3. Harold Klemp, *The Spiritual Exercises of ECK*, 2d ed. (Minneapolis: ECKANKAR, 1993, 1997), 129.

Chapter 4. Adventures in Dream Travel and Soul Travel

1. Harold Klemp, *The Eternal Dreamer*, Mahanta Transcripts, Book 7 (Minneapolis: ECKANKAR, 1992), 198.
2. Harold Klemp, *The Living Word*, Book 2 (Minneapolis: ECKANKAR, 1996), 137.
3. Klemp, *Past Lives, Dreams, and Soul Travel*, 152–54.
4. Klemp, *What Is Spiritual Freedom?* 161–62.
5. Harold Klemp, *ECK Masters and You: An Illustrated Guide* (Minneapolis: ECKANKAR, 2006), 63.

Chapter 5. Soul Travel and Past Lives

1. Harold Klemp, *The Slow Burning Love of God*, Mahanta Transcripts, Book 13, 2d ed. (Minneapolis: ECKANKAR, 1996, 1997), 174.
2. Luke 9:8 Authorized (King James) Version.

Chapter 6. Young Soul Travel Experts

1. Harold Klemp, *The Secret of Love*, Mahanta Transcripts, Book 14 (Minneapolis: ECKANKAR, 1996), 96.
2. Eugene Field, *Wynken, Blynken, and Nod*, in *An American Anthology, 1787–1900*, ed. Edmund Clarence Stedman (n.p., n.d.).
3. Harold Klemp, *The Secret of Love*, 96.

Chapter 7. Beyond Soul Travel—Living in Heaven Now

1. Harold Klemp, *The Dream Master*, Mahanta Transcripts, Book 8, 2d ed. (Minneapolis: ECKANKAR, 1993, 1997), 129.
2. Klemp, *The Art of Spiritual Dreaming*, 44.
3. Harold Klemp, *The Spiritual Laws of Life* (Minneapolis: ECKANKAR, 2002).
4. Klemp, *How to Survive Spiritually in Our Times*, 226–27.
5. Klemp, *The Art of Spiritual Dreaming*, 45.
6. Luke 12:31 Authorized (King James) Version.

7. Luke 17:21 Authorized (King James) Version.
8. Klemp, *The Art of Spiritual Dreaming*, 284.

Discover spiritual truth through past lives, dreams, and Soul Travel
Free Eckankar book reveals how

A seeker from New York wrote, "I received your packet and read your book, which was extremely helpful to me. Thank you."

Hundreds of thousands of people around the globe have read *ECKANKAR—Ancient Wisdom for Today* in more than eleven languages. And so many have benefited spiritually.

A Florida newspaper praised this book: "Fascinating and well worth reading as you bring deeper spiritual insight into your life."

You'll see how **past lives** affect every aspect of your life. The way you handle relationships. Make choices. Face challenges.

You'll learn through your own experience that **dreams** are real. They help you make better decisions. Lose the fear of dying—and living—by understanding them.

Using a special technique, you'll find how **Soul Travel** is a natural method for intuitively seeing the big picture and discover spiritual truth for yourself. Begin the adventure of a lifetime *today*.

To get your free copy of *ECKANKAR—Ancient Wisdom for Today* (a $4.95 value), go to Eckankar's Web site at

www.Eckankar.org
or call ☎ 1-800-LOVE GOD
(1-800-568-3463)
toll free, 24 hours a day. Ask for book #BK63.

Or you can write to: ECKANKAR, Dept. BK63, PO Box 2000, Chanhassen, MN 55317-2000 USA.

For Further Reading and Study

Those Wonderful ECK Masters
Harold Klemp

Could you be one of the countless people who have been touched by a meeting with an ECK Master? These real-life stories and spiritual exercises can awaken you to the presence and help of these spiritual guides. Since the beginning of time they have offered guidance, protection, and divine love to help you fulfill your spiritual destiny.

How to Survive Spiritually in Our Times, Mahanta Transcripts, Book 16
Harold Klemp

A master storyteller, Harold Klemp weaves stories, tips, and techniques into the golden fabric of his talks. They highlight the deeper truths within you, so you can apply them in your life *now*. He speaks right to Soul. It is that divine, eternal spark that you are. The survivor. Yet survival is only the starting point in your spiritual life. Harold Klemp also shows you how to gain in spiritual wealth. This book's a treasure.

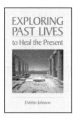

Exploring Past Lives to Heal the Present
Debbie Johnson

Threads from past lives may be intertwined with your present life. The teachings of ECK can help unlock the mysteries of our lives today. See how people like yourself have solved problems by learning about past-life influences. Explore who you are now, and take charge of your life!

Dreams: Your Window to Heaven
Debbie Johnson

Venture in your dreams to the limits of your imagination, even to the threshold of heaven. Explore your distant past, understand your present, and see future possibilities. Learn dynamic techniques and tips to mine the gold in your dreams; deal with nightmares; solve problems; review past lives; and have prophetic dreams by choice—not by chance.

Available at bookstores, online booksellers, or directly from Eckankar: www.Eckankar.org; (952) 380-2222; ECKANKAR, Dept. BK63, PO Box 2000, Chanhassen, MN 55317-2000 USA.

There May Be an
Eckankar Study Group near You

Eckankar offers a variety of local and international activities for the spiritual seeker. With hundreds of study groups worldwide, Eckankar is near you! Many areas have Eckankar centers where you can browse through the books in a quiet, unpressured environment, talk with others who share an interest in this ancient teaching, and attend beginning discussion classes on how to gain the attributes of Soul: wisdom, power, love, and freedom.

Around the world, Eckankar study groups offer special one-day or weekend seminars on the basic teachings of Eckankar. For membership information, visit the Eckankar Web site (www.Eckankar.org). For the location of the Eckankar center or study group nearest you, click on "Eckankar in Your Area" for a listing of those areas with Web sites. You're also welcome to check your phone book under **ECKANKAR**; call **(952) 380-2222, Ext. BK63;** or write **ECKANKAR, Att: Information, BK63, PO Box 2000, Chanhassen, MN 55317-2000 USA.**

☐ Please send me information on the nearest Eckankar center or study group in my area.

☐ Please send me more information about membership in Eckankar, which includes a twelve-month spiritual study.

Please type or print clearly

Name _____
    first (given)   last (family)

Street_____ Apt. # _____

City _____ State/Prov. _____

Zip/Postal Code _____ Country _____